FROM KORTI TO KHARTUM

FROM

KORTI TO KHARTUM

A JOURNAL OF THE DESERT MARCH FROM
KORTI TO GUBAT, AND OF THE ASCENT
OF THE NILE IN GENERAL
GORDON'S STEAMERS

COL. SIR CHARLES W. WILSON,

K.C.B., K.C.M.G., D.C.L., F.R.S., R.E.
DEPUTY ADJUTANT-GENERAL (INTELLIGENCE
BRANCH) NILE EXPEDITION

The Naval & Military Press Ltd

published in association with

FIREPOWER
The Royal Artillery Museum
Woolwich

Published by
The Naval & Military Press Ltd
Unit 10 Ridgewood Industrial Park,
Uckfield, East Sussex,
TN22 5QE England
Tel: +44 (0) 1825 749494
Fax: +44 (0) 1825 765701
www.naval-military-press.com

in association with

FIREPOWER
The Royal Artillery Museum, Woolwich
www.firepower.org.uk

The Naval & Military
Press

MILITARY HISTORY AT YOUR
FINGERTIPS

... a unique and expanding series of reference works

Working in collaboration with the foremost
regiments and institutions, as well as acknowledged
experts in their field, N&MP have assembled a
formidable array of titles including technologically
advanced CD-ROMs and facsimile reprints of
impossible-to-find rarities.

PREFACE.

THE Journal of the march from Korti to
Gubat, and of the voyage in General Gordon's steamers to the junction of the two
Niles, forms part of a daily journal which
I kept whilst employed in the Sudan, and
sent home by nearly every mail. It was
written up from the field-notes after my
return to Korti whilst all the events which
it describes were fresh in my memory. It
was hastily written amidst many interrup-
tions; sometimes the rough field-notes were
copied; sometimes they were corrected to

agree with more recent information. In preparing the Journal for publication, I have omitted several passages which were of interest only to myself and to my friends; and I have made many verbal alterations, which were rendered necessary by the haste with which it was written. The Journal was not written with a view to publication; but on my return to England, some friends, who had seen it, strongly advised me to publish, as they thought that some fuller account of the attempt to reach Khartum in General Gordon's steamers than has yet appeared should be given to the public. My reluctance to publish has delayed its appearance.

I thought at the time that, if we had reached Khartum before it fell, the presence of two armed steamers with a small detachment of British soldiers (twenty) might have turned the scale in General Gordon's favour. The fuller knowledge which I now possess of the condition of the garrison, and of the determination of the Mahdi to attack Khartum before the English arrived, leads me to believe that if the steamers had left Gubat a week earlier, the result would have been the same; and that even if it had been possible for them to have reached Khartum on the 25th January, their presence would not have averted the fall of the city.

The failure of the Relief Expedition to attain its object was deeply and sincerely regretted by every one in the force—by no one more so than by myself, for General Gordon was not only a brother officer but a personal friend. It failed; but, to quote Lord Wolseley's words, "this was from no lack of courage or of discipline, of dash or of endurance; . . . all ranks worked as hard as human beings could, hoping to render the earliest possible assistance to their heroic comrade who was besieged in Khartum."

C. W. WILSON.

DUBLIN, *October* 31, 1885.

CONTENTS.

b

BIVOUAC ON THE NILE.

IN FRONT OF MATAMMEH.

GUBAT TO SHENDY AND BACK.

GUBAT TO OMDURMAN.

INTRODUCTION.

On the 16th December 1884, Lord Wolseley reached Korti, and joined the camp which had been established on the previous day by Brigadier-General Sir Herbert Stewart. The troops then in camp were the Guards Camel Regiment, the Mounted Infantry Camel Regiment, and detachments of the South Staffordshire Regiment and of the Royal Engineers.

The latest direct news from General Gordon that the Expedition possessed at that time, was contained in a letter,[1] dated

[1] Appendix I.

November 4th, which had been brought
by one of Major Kitchener's messengers,
who had succeeded in entering Khartum
on the 3d, and in returning to Debbeh
on the 14th November. In his letter
General Gordon gave the following important information : "At Matammeh, waiting
your orders, are five steamers with nine
guns." "We can hold out forty days with
ease ; after that it will be difficult." "The
Mahdi is here, about eight miles away.
All north side along the White Nile is
free of Arabs ; they are on south and south-
west and east of town some way off; they
are quiet." "I should take the road from
Ambukol to Matammeh, where my steamers
wait for you." On the back of the letter
there was a small plan showing the distribution of the Mahdi's army (20,000
men), and the number and position of his

guns. Previous to our arrival at Korti we had heard of the presence of five of General Gordon's steamers at Shendy; of the fighting round Khartum; of the frequent desertions from the Mahdi to General Gordon; of the sickness and want of food in the Mahdi's camp; of the defection of some of the Baggara Arabs; and of other details which are mentioned in General Gordon's Journal. There had been some raiding in the desert between Debbeh and Khartum, but no roving bands had been reported in the desert between Korti and Matammeh.

Between the 16th and 30th of December the camp at Korti presented a busy scene: troops were arriving daily by land and river; preparations were being made for the desert march; and the advanced boats of the river column were being sent on to Belal, at the foot of the Gerendid Cataract.[1] During this interval additional details were received with regard to the fighting round Khartum, and we heard that Gordon's steamers had recently been up to the city with provisions;[2] that there was a force with firearms at Matammeh; and that the Mudir of Bahr Ghazal (supposed to be Lupton Bey) had surrendered and been sent to Obeid. We also obtained, through our own agents, information respecting the strength and distribution of the Mahdi's army round Khartum, which agreed very closely with that given by General Gordon.

On the 30th December, Sir Herbert Stewart left with the Camel Corps to occupy the wells of Jakdul. On the 31st,

---

[1] This name is not known in the country. I have retained it here as it has become familiar from its adoption on the War Department map used during the expedition.

[2] This report apparently referred to the 'Bordein,' which left Khartum on the 14th December.

a messenger, who had been sent to General Gordon on the 29th October, returned.
He brought a piece of paper, the size of
a postage - stamp, on which was written
"Khartoum all right"; it was signed
C. G. Gordon, and dated December 14,
1884. The messenger was told to deliver
a verbal message,[1] of which the following
is the most important portion: "The
enemy cannot take us except by starving
us out. Our troops suffer from want of
provisions; the food we still have is little—
some grain and biscuit. We want you to
come quickly. Do not scatter your troops;
the enemy is numerous; bring plenty of
troops if you can. You should come by
way of Matammeh or Berber; only by these
two roads. Do not leave Berber in your
rear. Keep the enemy in your front; and

[1] See Parliamentary Paper, Egypt, No. 1 (1885), p. 132.

when you take Berber send me word, and
come by the east bank. Do this without
letting rumours of your approach spread
abroad." The messenger also stated that
General Gordon's steamers had gone up
the river to Wady Bishara to collect the
crops on the islands in the cataract.[1]

On New Year's Day the first boats of the
Black Watch reached Korti; on the 3d January General Earle, who had arrived on the
1st, left to join the advanced-guard of his
force; and on the 4th, the South Staffordshire Regiment passed the Gerendid
Cataract, and occupied Hamdab, where the
river column was to assemble before making
a forward movement. On the 5th, Lord
Charles Beresford reached Korti with the
First Division of the Naval Brigade; and

---

[1] The steamers were really at Nasri Island, some distance
below Wady Bishara.

on the same day Sir Herbert Stewart
returned from Jakdul, where he had left
the Guards Camel Regiment. The march
of the latter had been most successful;
it had taken the enemy completely by
surprise; and there had been no opposition. The camels, with a few exceptions,
looked little the worse for their forced
march to Jakdul and back; but some of
us, who had had previous experience of
the "ship of the desert," were afraid that
more had been taken out of them than
was apparent to the eye. Several prisoners, Awadiyeh Arabs from the neighbourhood of Matammeh, were brought in;
they were not very communicative, but
they confirmed the report that there was
a force at Matammeh armed with rifles,
and that General Gordon's steamers were
on the river below the cataract.

On the 7th January the Light Camel Regiment, under the command of Colonel Stanley Clarke, left for Jakdul with a convoy of 1000 camels; and on the 8th, Sir Herbert Stewart's force commenced its march across the desert. Sir Herbert Stewart's instructions [1] were to attack and occupy Matammeh, and then to return to Jakdul, whence he was to continue forwarding stores to Matammeh. The force at his disposal consisted of—

First Division of the Naval Brigade.

One squadron of the 19th Hussars.

The Guards Camel Regiment,[2] composed of selected men from the three regiments of Guards, and from the Royal Marines.

The Heavy Camel Regiment, "the

[1] Appendix II.

[2] The organisation of the Camel Corps is given in Appendix III.

Heavies," composed of selected men
from the three Household and seven
other cavalry regiments.

The Mounted Infantry Camel Regiment,
composed of selected men from various
regiments, most of whom had served
with the Mounted Infantry in South
Africa or Egypt.

Half a battery Royal Artillery.

Detachment Royal Engineers.

400 men of the Royal Sussex Regiment
(old 35th), of whom 150 were to be
left at Jakdul.

One company of the Essex Regiment
(old 56th), destined to form a post
at Howeiyat.

The Bearer Company.

The Movable Field Hospital.

Transport details.

In all, about 120 officers and 1900 men,

with 300 natives, interpreters, camel-drivers, &c.

The Light Camel Regiment, " the Lights," composed of selected men from nine Cavalry regiments, was employed almost entirely on escort duty with convoys.

When the column left Korti on the 8th, the position was nearly as follows :—

British.—The river column assembling at Hamdab; Jakdul held by the Guards Camel Regiment; General Gordon's four steamers [1] on the Nile below the Shabloka Cataract; and Khartum and Omdurman holding out.

---

[1] No communication was received from the steamers; the commander, Nashi Pasha, appears to have made only one attempt to communicate with Lord Wolseley, and that failed. Messengers could have been sent from the steamers by Wady Bishara and Bayuda without much difficulty.

Enemy.—Birti held by the Monassir and dervishes from Berber; no one in the desert between Korti and Matammeh, except the Arabs living there; at Matammeh a force variously reported to be from 300 to 3000 men armed with rifles, and two guns; at Berber a force supposed to be small, but known to be partly armed with rifles, and two steamers; at Shendy a small force; and round Khartum the Mahdi's army of 20,000 men.

The plan of the Mahdi appears to have been to try and crush the British column at the end of its desert march; and as soon as the occupation of Jakdul was known, his troops were set in motion. The following dates show what occurred: Jakdul was occupied by Sir Herbert Stewart at 6.45 A.M. on the 2d January; on the 4th, Muhammed el Kheir, the Emir of Berber,

ordered his men to proceed to the assistance of the Emir of Matammeh.[1] Omdurman fell between the 6th and 13th, and
the battle of Abu Klea was fought on the
17th. The enemy had thus thirteen days
to concentrate his troops at Abu Klea.
Matammeh, the immediate objective of the
British column, was 176 miles from Korti,
and only about 90 miles from Berber, and
98 miles from Khartum.

The country between Korti and Matammeh is not a desert in the true sense of the
term. After the first twenty miles from
Korti, there is an abundant supply of
savas grass, excellent food for camels, at
short intervals, and a fair quantity of
wood—acacia and mimosa. There is good
water at Howeiyat, Abu Halfa, Jakdul, and
Abu Klea, as well as in some of the ravines

[1] Appendix IV.

in Jebel Jilif; and water would probably
be found by digging in many of the dry
water-courses. The torrents which descend
from Jebel Jilif during the rainy season,
have formed an alluvial plain, a few miles
to the south-west of the road, on which
crops of dura are raised every year;
and judging from the numerous tracks
seen, the Arabs of this district must
possess large herds of cattle. The road
throughout is excellent; there are no hills;
the country is open; and, with the exception of a few patches of sand between Jakdul and Abu Klea, the ground is firm, and
presents no difficulty to the passage of
troops whether mounted or on foot.

The weather, up to the end of February,
was almost perfect; the nights cold, and
the mid-day heat always tempered by a
cool breeze.

JOURNAL.

Jan. 8, 1885. — In the morning I received Lord Wolseley's instructions[1] for Gordon and myself, which had been read to me yesterday. In the afternoon I joined Herbert Stewart's column[2] with Dickson of the Royals, who was to be left at Khartum with Gordon, and Verner, Rifle Brigade, who was to sketch the road, and be left at Matammeh as intelligence officer. The column formed up on the desert behind the village of Korti, and after having been inspected by Lord Wolseley, moved off about

[1] Appendix V.   [2] Appendix VI.

A

two. We were all in high spirits at commencing, at last, the real business of the
campaign, and started with many good
wishes for success from those we left behind.
We camped in the desert a little after sunset, in a long line, headquarters and advanced-guard in the centre, with the other
divisions to the right and left. Outposts
were thrown out, fires lighted, suppers
cooked and eaten, and then we lay down
to sleep, with *réveillé* at 12.30 A.M. to dream
of.

Jan. 9th.—We had not much rest after
all, for Dickson's camel broke loose, and
started off, with Dickson, Verner, and servants in hot pursuit. They first went over
the " Heavies," then doubled back on headquarters, and finally finished their hunt in
the Naval Brigade. I think they roused
up pretty nearly every one, and they were
followed by a copious flow of that strong
language which Tommy Atkins has in-

herited from his forefathers who fought in Flanders. By the time we had had a cup of chocolate the moon was well up, and there was a good light; yet as we were waiting for the order to march, Dickson and I with the guides a little in front of the centre, the whole of the right wing marched across our front, in a direction nearly at right angles to our proper road. Who originated the movement I never heard, but it caused a long delay and some confusion. It was cold enough before daylight to make ulsters and jerseys acceptable, but very enjoyable, and the sky was more than usually fine with moon, Venus, Southern Cross, False Cross, Sirius, Orion, Great Bear, and Pole-star above the horizon at the same time. The great column moving silently along under the moonlight was a sight not easily forgotten. Our marches yesterday and this morning had been over firm gravelly ground with sparse

vegetation, a little grass, and a few mimosa;
but a little before ten we reached Wady Abu
Gir, where there was abundance of grass
and numbers of mimosa. We halted four
hours for breakfast and rest, and then went
on again until sunset, when we reached a
valley with good grass for grazing : there
was not much chance, however, for the
camels, as they were all tied down tightly
directly they came in, and had no time for
grazing. Very hot in middle of day, but
more from reflection upwards than from
direct rays of sun. All went well, and the
sailors, with Beresford on his white donkey,
in high spirits, very amusing and nautical.
" Quartermaster, can't you make that gun
sit a little better on the camel ? " " Can't,
sir; camel's got his hump all a-starboard,"
was the ready reply.

Jan. 10*th.* — Started in the dark, and
much straggling of camels in consequence.
One of the native camel-drivers managed to

drink all the water out of my water-skin, which was lying close beside me, and another succeeded in stealing my water-bottle: rather bad losses for the second night in the desert. Some of the Sussex Regiment were short of water, and suffered a good deal. They had come up to Korti in boats, and had their camels and water-skins given to them only two or three days before starting; many of the skins were bad and leaky. Missed our way twice in the dark this morning; several things left behind, including a camel with its entire load. The drivers slip loads unseen in the dark; and it saves them trouble afterwards.

Soon after daylight we reached the wells of Hambok, in an open valley where there was much vegetation—tall "savas" grass and mimosa-bushes. There were only a few cupfuls of water in the wells, so we continued to El Howeiyat, about nine miles farther on. By the time we got there it

was very hot, and many of the men were
suffering much from thirst. I rode on in
front, and found the wells had been drained
by Stanley Clarke's column, the end of
which I just saw crossing a hill in the distance. Our column was halted a short distance from the wells, and some of the reserve water was served out for breakfast;
sentries were then placed over the wells,
and as they gradually filled, the men were
marched up by companies to have a drink
of the pure but muddy water. The men
behaved very well, but it was difficult to
keep the natives in order; however, they
were better than the Egyptian soldiers with
Stanley Clarke, who, I was told, almost
mutinied.

In the afternoon we started for Abu
Halfa, as we were too short of water to go
on to Jakdul. Just after sunset fires were
seen in the distance, which Stewart took to
be Stanley Clarke's camp-fires; and wishing

to pass him, he continued the march long
after dark over some rough country. Finally,
in trying to get round the camp, the head
of the column came right up against some
rough stony ground. We were at once
halted, and bivouacked in column as we
had marched. The way in which the unfortunate camels tumbled about in the dark,
and loads came off, and the strong language
that was used, were things to see and hear.
The column got mixed up in the dark, and
it was over an hour before our servants
reached the head of the column with something to eat. After all, the camp turned
out to be that of Barrow and the 19th
Hussars, who had left us at Howeiyat and
marched straight on to avoid the tiring
halts.

Jan. 11*th.* — Want of water much felt
last night by the Sussex and some others.
March in the dark with usual confusion and
false start, part of the column moving off

in the wrong direction before the guides. Barrow pushed on with his horses, as water was necessary for their existence; and a very thirsty column followed him to the wells of Abu Halfa, where we found much less water than we expected. There was one pond of dirty water almost black with mud, and a few holes in the gravel with better water. We set to work to open new holes, into which the water ran quickly; but the men were so wild with thirst that, directly the water began running in, we had to give the holes up to them and begin digging others. The men behaved admirably. Officers and men were marched up, and each received a pint; they then moved off to their camping-grounds, and were afterwards allowed to come and draw water for cooking. We managed to get three tin biscuit-boxes sunk in the ground, to act as rough filters and reservoirs, from which the men could bale out water; but it

was hard work. It was a curious scene, as
the camels, donkeys, and ponies rushed for
the water directly they arrived, and had to
be kept back by main force. All the afternoon there was a continuous stream of
men going down for water, and it was kept
up the whole night. Some of the officers
worked hard in the hot sun digging new
wells and distributing water to all comers.
The Mounted Infantry, all old soldiers,
looked after by picked officers, did not
suffer at all. They had as much as they
wished to drink on the road, and brought
in a large quantity of spare water. This
shows what can be done with a little
management. The Abu Halfa valley is
prettily wooded, and the granite hills towards its head are more broken and diver-
sified than any we have yet seen.

Some talk with —— about the night-
marches, as to which we differ. He says
truly that the camels march much better

at night, and that men and camels suffer
from the heat when they march by day.
I contend that sleep by day is not so re-
freshing as sleep by night for the men;
that when the camels are loaded in the
dark the loads are badly put on, and that
sore backs are started before the loads can
be properly adjusted by daylight; that
owing to the constant long halts, necessary
to keep the column together in the dark,
the loads remain on the camels' backs for
an excessively long time, fifteen or sixteen
hours out of the twenty-four; that the
camels start on empty stomachs, contrary
to the habit of the beast; that much harm
is done to the camels by marching, in close
order, in the dark over rough ground; that
the camels get neither proper rest nor food;
and that men cannot stand marching from
2 A.M. to 10 or 11 A.M. with nothing inside them. I cannot think why we violate
all the dictates of common-sense in our

treatment of the camel, and believe we should get much more out of ours if we worked them more as the Arabs do. The desert is not a desert in the proper sense of the term. There is ample water, abundant vegetation, and an almost limitless supply of savas grass, the best of feeding for camels; and here ours are failing before we have commenced, simply because we will not give them time to feed, and when in camp tie them down so tightly they cannot move. I do not think more than 500 camels should ever travel together, and 300 would be a safer limit. It would be heresy to say the camelry is a mistake; but if Tommy Atkins cannot march in such a climate as this, we had better give up fighting.

Jan. 12th.—This morning, as we had only a short march to make, we did not load up until daylight, and those who were not over-thirsty had a good night's rest.

Our road lay at the foot of the long range
of Jebel Jilif, which is broken by numerous
ravines, in nearly all of which there is
water; at times there must be heavy rain-
storms, as the torrent-beds are well marked
a long way out on the plain. We reached
Jakdul in good time, and found it a very
curious place. Leaving the plain, we turned
up a wide valley with good grass, and then
turning to the left, passed through a narrow
opening into a sort of punch-bowl, or crater-
like place, into which three or four ravines
drained : in one of these are the two pools,
one level with the floor of the punch-bowl,
with water only fit for camels, the other
higher up, with pure fresh water. The
Guards had been left by Stewart to hold the
wells after his seizure of them, and we were
surprised at the amount of work they had
done. Two stone forts had been built, the
ground had been laid out for us to camp
on, paths made, and signboards put up, so

that we easily fell into our places. Dorward and Lawson, R.E., had been working
hard at the watering arrangements. They
had made a small canal, into which water
was pumped for the camels; and a reservoir
of biscuit-tins, into which water was pumped
from above, for the men. It did not, however, come fast enough for the thirsty crowd
that came in; and all the afternoon there
was a string of men going up and down the
rock to and from the upper pool, whence
they had to draw the water with buckets
and ropes, as it is surrounded on all sides,
except the lowest, by cliffs. I passed most
of the afternoon with Kitchener, who had
established himself in a cave on the side of
the hill. He had caught several men carrying dates to the enemy, but had little news
of any kind from the front, except that
Khashm el Mus was still at Shendy with
three steamers,[1] and that there were 300 men

[1] He was really at Nasri Island, below Wady Bishara.

at Matammeh under Wad Sad, the Mahdi's Emir; he had sent out messengers, but none had returned. He was very sore at the order I brought him to return to Korti with Stanley Clarke's convoy. In the evening the Guards gave us a capital dinner, to which we did full justice. Gordon Cumming had had his usual success amongst the gazelle, and many sand-grouse had been secured as well, so there was a pleasant change from "bully" beef, and the thirst which it begets.

Jan. 13*th.*—A busy scene all day watering camels, filling up water-tanks, and organising the convoy for the onward march to-morrow. The Guards had to be remounted, as they had been obliged to send back their camels to bring up the Sussex Regiment and stores. The supply of camels is much too small, and we are already beginning to feel the effect of the fast-and-loose game played with regard to the purchase of camels in October, November, and December. At one time an order came, buy away; then stop buying; then again, buy away,—and so on. Carmichael, 5th Lancers, who was on watering duty last night, told me he had never seen such a curious scene as that at the upper pool, where the men were drawing water all night by the light of lanterns; luckily, no one fell in. Jakdul is not a pleasant place. It is a regular frying-pan; the rocks get heated up, and there is no breeze, but about 2 A.M. a hurricane comes down the hillside, and nearly pulls the blanket off one; then it gets quite cold till sunrise, when the caldron heats up again. Stuart-Wortley joined me for service at Khartum with Gordon. Burnaby also came in with a convoy, and brought Gascoigne,[1] whom he

[1] Captain Gascoigne had previously travelled in the Eastern Sudan, and collected much information respecting the country on the Abyssinian frontier, which he had placed at the disposal of the War Department.

introduced to me as "a young man who
knew his way about in the Sudan." All
day long the same busy scene at the wells,
watering camels and filling up water-tanks
for the journey.

Jan. 14*th.*—Stanley Clarke left early in
the morning with the return convoy for
Korti, Kitchener going with him, much to his
disgust. The Guards went on with us, and
Colonel Vandeleur was left with a strong
detachment of the Sussex to hold the wells.
We formed up, with our unwieldy convoy,
a little before 2 P.M. in the valley outside
the Jakdul crater, and travelled for about
three hours. Just before we started a Rem-
ington rifle was found on the rocks close by,
the first trace of an enemy we have seen.
As we got out on to the desert, however,
we saw some recent horse-tracks a little off
the road to Matammeh, so it was clear our
advance was known.

Jan. 15*th.* — Started at daylight, and

passed over a tract of loose sand where the track was occasionally quite covered by drift-sand. It was not, however, nearly so bad as we expected to find it, and there is such a good landmark in an isolated hill of sandstone that no one could lose his way. During the day we saw very distinctly the recent tracks of horses passing to and from Matammeh, evidently those of some of the enemy's scouts who had been watching us, and in the distance we saw three or four of their camel-men. We have no news from the front, and have met none of our messengers coming back. We camped for the night near Jebel Sergain, the camels tied down, and everything prepared for an attack should one be made. In one or two places the country was prettily wooded, and for a long distance there was an abundance of savas grass ; but alas ! the camels had no opportunity of eating it, and the supply of dura we could carry was but small.

B

Jan. 16*th.* — This morning we started
before daylight with the usual result. As
I was waiting with the guides for orders to
start, a part of the column went away to
the left, out into the darkness, and it was
over half an hour before they got into their
places again; then we got into some rough
ground with high tufts of grass, amongst
which the camels tumbled about. Here
there were more halts and delays, and fully
an hour was lost altogether, during which
the camels had their loads on. When daylight broke we found ourselves on a vast
plain, scantily covered with savas grass,
with the hills of Abu Klea in front of us in
the distance. Barrow was ordered to push
on with his Hussars and occupy the wells,
and with him rode Dickson and Stuart-
Wortley; we followed more leisurely with
our camels. Between ten and eleven, just
before reaching the foot of the hills, we
halted for breakfast, and about eleven Bar-

row reported that he had found the enemy
in force between us and the wells.   One of
his officers had a narrow escape.   He had
started with three or four hussars in pursuit of some of the enemy's scouts, and
followed them into the Abu Klea valley,
where he actually caught hold of one
man; but a lot of spearmen jumping up
from the long grass, he had to drop his
prisoner and ride for his life.   After breakfast we all mounted, much excited at the
idea of a fight.   After ascending the pass
which leads to the Abu Klea wells, I went
out with Stewart to see what could be seen
of the enemy.   After a short time he returned to select a good place to halt the
convoy, and I went on to reconnoitre, first
to some hills on the left, whence about fifty
horsemen could be seen, and then to the
advanced picket of hussars down the valley.
From this latter point I could see a long
line of banners fluttering in the breeze and

stretching right across the road. There was
a large tent, and we could hear the "tom-
toms" or war-drums beating vigorously,
whilst some white puffs of smoke in the
distance showed that their riflemen were
firing at us. It was, however, too far, and
no bullet reached us. I then returned to
Stewart and told him that he had a large
force in front of him, of which part at least
must belong to the Mahdi's army, and that
he would have something more serious to
deal with than desert Arabs. I found he had
halted the column on a stony plateau. He
now gave orders to form a zeribah, and sent
pickets out to occupy two hills on our left.
I then went back to the hussar post where
I had left Dickson, and found the enemy's
riflemen were creeping up on the right, and
that there was some movement amongst
the men in the valley. Stewart soon afterwards came out, and as the afternoon was
getting on, determined not to advance until

the morning. The riflemen who had been creeping round on the hills to our right now got within range, and Dickson and I began to hear the whistle of bullets about our heads. At first the bullets were few and far between, but they gradually increased until they got too numerous for the picket, which was in an exposed position and had to be withdrawn. The riflemen still kept working round our right, and as they advanced the cavalry vedettes were withdrawn. It was nearly sunset when we got into the zeribah, and by this time a party of the enemy's sharpshooters had established themselves on a high hill to our right, from which they opened fire. Just before dark they got the range pretty well, and a man of the Hussars and several horses and camels were hit. All night long they kept up their fire, but luckily it was very dark, and there were few casualties; the whistling of the bullets overhead was, however, too

near to be pleasant, and the vagaries of
the tom-toms in the valley, which now approached and now retired, kept us constantly on the alert. I do not know a
more curiously deceptive sound than that of
tom-toms ; it is almost impossible to localise
it, especially when any wind is blowing. I
slept near Stewart and his staff, close behind the Guards, who were in the front
line of the zeribah, and in one of the lines
of fire; fortunately there was a little dip
in the ground which sheltered us, the
bullets striking the opposite slope—thus.

We slept at *A*, and the bullets kept striking
the ground at *B*.

Jan. 17*th.*—The enemy must have kept
a sharp look-out last night, for as one of the
surgeons was performing an operation in
the hospital, the man holding the lantern

incautiously turned it towards the hill occupied by the riflemen; a volley of bullets
was the immediate answer, succeeded by a
steady fire, which luckily did little harm.
An attack was expected in the morning,
and we all stood to our arms as Venus rose,
that being the signal by which we had heard
the Arabs generally attacked. We waited
thus till daylight, when the fire from the
hills became hotter, and some of the Guards
and Mounted Infantry were sent out as skirmishers to keep it down. Several of the
enemy showed great boldness, running down
the hill and creeping up towards the zeribah,
whilst others kept on firing from the hill,
where they were well protected by low
stone walls. Stewart had talked about
occupying this hill last evening, but thought
it too far off for the enemy to do us any
harm; we did not realise that we had such
good shots in front of us. We could see
that the enemy in the valley had come

much nearer to us during the night, and
the tent had disappeared, but they showed
in no large masses. We waited some time,
hoping they might attack us, and a few
officers and men were hit near the point
B: first Gough, commanding the Mounted
Infantry, who was hit on the side of the
head, the bullet passing through his helmet
and puggery, but not breaking the skin—
a very narrow escape; then Dickson, shot
through the leg just below the knee. I was
standing at the time close to the Guards,
and went over to him as soon as I heard
of it. It was bad luck to get hit so
early in the first fight; but what he felt
most was, that it was now impossible for
him to go on to Khartum with me. He
was very cheery as he was carried off to
hospital, but anxious to know what the
report on his wound would be. Some
horsemen now came round our right, but
they were soon dispersed by a few rounds

of shell; and as it became evident that the
enemy intended to keep up a harassing fire
on us, and not deliver an attack, Stewart
determined to march out and give battle,
leaving a force behind to hold the zeribah.
The square was then formed up, and we
marched down the valley towards the row
of flags which stretched across it, whilst
Barrow with the cavalry moved off to the
left to keep the enemy on the hills in
check. The square was formed up thus :
Guards and Mounted Infantry in front, the

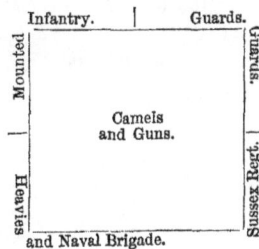

Heavies and Sussex Regiment in rear, and
the Naval Brigade with the Heavies. As
we moved on, the firing continued, and

St Vincent, adjutant of the Heavies, was
badly hit. We halted several times and
returned the fire with Martinis and the
screw guns : these had some effect, for we
could see numbers of men streaming off
from the enemy's right in the valley. We
kept to the right until we got out of the
grass and had clear ground round us; and
then moved on, with Campbell's company
of Mounted Infantry out as skirmishers on
our left front. When the skirmishers got
within about 200 yards of the flags, the
square was halted for the rear to close

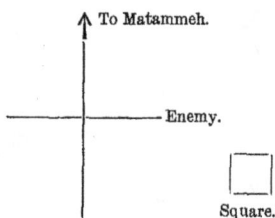

up, and at this moment the enemy rose
from the ravine in which they were hidden,
in the most perfect order. It was a beauti-

ful and striking sight, such a one as Fitz-
James must have seen when Roderick Dhu's
men rose out of the heather; nothing could
be more applicable than Scott's description.
How they managed to conceal their horses
I know not, but they did so very effectually.
The formation was curious, a sort of variety
of the old phalanx. It was as if there were
portions of three phalanxes with rows of

Front.

```
   .        .        .
  ...      ...      ...
 ....     ....     ....
.....    .....    .....
......   ......   ......
.....................
.....................
.....................
```

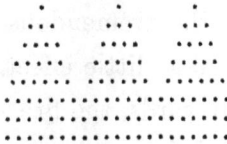

men behind. At the head of each rode an
emir or sheikh with a banner, accompanied by personal attendants, and then came
the fighting men. They advanced at a quick
even pace as if on parade, and our skirmishers had only just time to get into the
square before they were upon us : one poor
fellow who lagged behind was caught and

speared at once. When the enemy commenced their advance, I remember experi-
encing a feeling of pity mixed with admiration for them, as I thought they would all
be shot down in a few minutes. I could
not have believed beforehand that men in
close formation would have been able to
advance for 200 to 400 yards over bare
ground in the face of Martini-Henrys. As
they advanced the feeling was changed to
wonder that the tremendous fire we were
keeping up had so little effect. When they
got within 80 yards, the fire of the Guards
and Mounted Infantry began to take good
effect, and a huge pile of dead rose in front
of them. Then to my astonishment the enemy took ground to their right as if on parade, so as to envelop the rear of the square.
I remember thinking, "By Jove, they will be
into the square!" and almost the next moment I saw a fine old sheikh on horseback
plant his banner in the centre of the square,

behind the camels. He was at once shot down, falling on his banner. He turned out to be Musa, Emir of the Duguaim Arabs, from Kordofan. I had noticed him in the advance, with his banner in one hand and a book of prayers in the other, and never saw anything finer. The old man never swerved to the right or left, and never ceased chanting his prayers until he had planted his banner in our square. If any man deserved a place in the Moslem Paradise, he did. When I saw the old sheikh in the square, and heard the wild uproar behind the camels, I drew my revolver; for directly the sheikh fell, the Arabs began running in under the camels to the front part of the square. Some of the rear rank now faced about and began firing. By this fire Herbert Stewart's horse was shot, and as he fell three Arabs ran at him. I was close to his horse's tail, and disposed of the one nearest to me, about three paces off; and the others were, I think, killed by the Mounted Infantry officers close by. Almost immediately afterwards the enemy retired, and loud and long cheering broke out from the square. Our men had by this time got somewhat out of hand, wild with excitement. It was for a few moments difficult to get them into their places; and if the enemy had charged again, few of us would have escaped. At one time this seemed likely, as they retired slowly, and for a short time hesitated in the valley before they made their final bolt. During this period of excitement, groups of three to five Arabs who had feigned death would start up from the slain and rush wildly at the square. They were met by a heavy fire, but so badly directed that several of them got right up to the bayonets. The men did not quiet down until the square was re-formed on the gravel-slope, about fifty yards in advance of the spot where it had stood to meet the attack. Many of the officers and men now went out to bring in water-skins and ammunition-boxes from the camels which had been killed. Curious how one's feelings get blunted by the sight of blood and horrors. There was one strange incident. An unwounded Arab, armed with a spear, jumped up and charged an officer. The officer grasped the spear with his left hand, and with his right ran his sword through the Arab's body; and there for a few seconds they stood, the officer being unable to withdraw his sword, until a man ran up and shot the Arab. It was a living embodiment of one of the old gladiatorial frescoes at Pompeii. It did not, strange to say, seem horrible; rather, after what had passed, an everyday occurrence. I used to wonder before how the Romans could look on at the gladiatorial fights; I do so no longer.

I went out to help about the water, &c.,
and found the spot where the square had
been broken a horrible sight—too horrible
for description. Carmichael was accident-
ally shot through the head by one of our
own men, so that death must have been
instantaneous. Gough of the Royals, and,
I fear, others, lost their lives in the same
way. How I escaped when the rear rank
turned round to fire I know not, except that
many of the men were so excited that they
fired up in the air. After I had been out
some time walking about, I had to come
back quite done up and lie flat on my
back, with my head in such shade as a
kneeling camel could give. I had marched
on foot from the zeribah, and the hot sun,
combined with the excitement of the fight,
and the work after, had, I suppose, knocked
me up. We all felt when it was over that
we had had a narrow escape. The camels
in the centre saved us, for they stopped the

rush of the Arabs, and thus gave the momentary check necessary for the rifles to do their work.

How was the square broken? you will say. Well, there are various opinions; one is, that it was a mistake to turn cavalry into infantry, and make them fight in square with an arm they were not accustomed to. Add to this, the cavalry were detachments from different regiments, only brought together a few days before we left Korti. A cavalry man is taught never to be still, and that a square can be broken. How can you expect him in a moment to forget all his training, stand like a rock, and believe no one can get inside a square? Then a cavalry man has a short handy carbine; he is given a long rifle and bayonet, and uses them for the first time in his life when a determined enemy is charging him. The Heavy Camel Corps had marched straight up from Assuan in detachments, and its organisation was changed from troops to companies only just before leaving Korti; it had also had little drill as infantry. Those who were near the Heavies told me that as the men fired they moved back involuntarily — not being taught, as infantry men are, to stand in a rigid line; they thus got clubbed together, and Burnaby tried to open them out so as to get a greater development of fire and let the Gardner play.[1] He saw at once, however, that it was too late, and riding out met his death like a gallant English gentleman. The Gardner got jammed at the tenth round, and the Arabs ran in at the opening, as they did at Tamai. The corner of the square had now got crushed in at *A*, and the men were so crowded they

---

[1] I was in the front part of the square, and could not see what occurred behind the camels. There was no want of steadiness on the part of the men, and their failure to deliver an effective fire appears to have been due to several causes.

could not deliver an effective fire. They
appear to have been pressed
back to higher ground at *B*,
where they rallied and poured
in a heavy fire on the Arabs, who had been
checked by the camels. It was all over in
five minutes, and the execution done by the
Arabs in that time with their spears was
extraordinary. Another cause of the disaster was the jamming of the cartridges,
which are made on economical principles,
and do not stand knocking about. I saw
myself several men throw their rifles down
with bitter curses when they found them
jammed and useless ; and if infantry did
this, the cavalry using the long rifle for the
first time must have been worse. Can you
imagine a more dreadful position than that
of being face to face with an Arab, and your
only arm a rifle that will not go off? The
sailors were pressed back with the cavalry
and lost heavily : they get very excited,
and would storm a work or do anything of

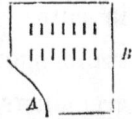

that kind well; but they are trained to fight
in ships, and you cannot expect them to
stand shoulder to shoulder in a square like
grenadiers. Their officers died, disdaining to
move from their gun, as they did at Tamai.
Many had narrow escapes. Verner was
knocked over by the rush, and saved by a
camel falling across him. Beresford was
also knocked over, as were several others.
I was much struck by the demeanour of the
Guards officers. There was no noise or fuss;
all the orders were given as if on parade,
and they spoke to their men in a quiet
manner, as if nothing unusual was going on.
——, when he found the Arabs had swept
past him, handed his company over to his
subaltern and rushed into the thick of the
fight round Burnaby. How he got out of
it without a scratch was a marvel to all.
The Mounted Infantry also did well, and
it was curious to contrast the huge pile of
dead in front of them with the small number in front of the cavalry. In the *mêlée*

that ensued, when the square was broken, the Heavies fought with the most determined bravery, and I was told that not a single Arab succeeded in passing through the ranks of the Life Guards and Blues.

Soon after the retreat of the Arabs, Barrow came up with his Hussars. He had seen the Arabs charge and retire, and had no idea that they had got into the square. Barrow had kept in check a large body of the enemy which had been trying to work round us; but his horses, after the march across the desert, were not in a fit state to act efficiently as cavalry. Stewart sent him on at once to occupy the Abu Klea wells. It was only by degrees that we realised how heavy our losses had been, not only in men but in camels.[1] After we had drawn off from the scene of the fight, we

---

[1] Sir Herbert Stewart's first impulse, when he realised the heavy losses which the force had sustained, was to halt at the Abu Klea wells for reinforcements. On further consideration, however, he decided to push on to the Nile next day.

found several boxes of ammunition for which there were no camels, and all the rifles of the killed and wounded men. A lot of the ammunition was burned, and many of the rifles broken, but several rifles and boxes of ammunition were left on the ground. The fire from the burning cartridges caught the pack-saddles of the dead and wounded camels and added to the horrors. A great collection of Mahdi's banners, swords, and spears was made, but, curiously enough, there were no shields, which the Kordofan Arabs do not seem to use.

At last the square began to move on to the wells. St Leger Herbert very kindly lent me his pony, so that I got on well enough; and after the square had gone a short distance, I rode down to the valley to see what traces the Arabs had left behind. I soon found that they had made a clean bolt, leaving nearly everything behind,

though that was not much. Stuart-Wortley
got a good prayer - carpet. There were
many donkeys, and several filled skins of
water which we sent up to the wounded in
the square. Here and there was a poor Arab
who had fallen dead in his flight. At last
a hussar came back from Barrow to say
that he had occupied the wells without
opposition. When I got to the first one I
had a good drink, and with the rest the
ride had given me, felt quite fresh again.

The wells are a series of pits in the sand
of the valley-bed, with little basins at the
bottom into which the water trickles. There
are great numbers of them, but some are
much better than others. In one of the pits
I found a couple of kids, which I at once
annexed for our own mess and Stewart's. I
found Barrow busy watering his horses, who
were wild with thirst; and then, when the
square came up, we set to work telling
off wells to the different regiments. The

men were very thirsty after the fight and
march in the sun, but behaved capitally,
and I had no difficulty in keeping the best
well clear for the hospital. Most of the
wounded had stood the journey well, but
poor St Vincent was terribly shaken. He
was in a cacolet on one' side of a camel, a
soldier being in one on the other side, when
the square was broken. The camel was
killed and fell on St Vincent, who was thus
saved, whilst the other wounded man was at
once speared. I had seen something of him
on the march, and admired his cheeriness
and readiness to do anything; and even
now, though so badly shaken and wounded,
he was quite cheery about himself. The
Hussars brought in a couple of wounded
men, who had to be examined, and a lot
of letters and papers found on the Arabs
were handed over to me, so that I had
plenty to do till dark. Soon after sunset a
strong detachment was sent back to the

zeribah, with orders to bring up the camels
and the commissariat stores as soon as they
could. We had little to eat except the biscuit we had put in our pockets, so that the
kid was very acceptable—and the water,
though muddy, was cool and sweet.

Jan. 18*th.*—I think few of us had any
sleep last night. We had no blankets or
greatcoats, and lay down as we were on the
sand. It was very cold all night, and bitterly
so in the early morning. Verner, Wortley,
and I tried to sleep under the prayer-carpet
Wortley had looted; and I think we spent
most of the time in trying to pull it off each
other, for none of us did more than doze for
a few moments at a time. About an hour
and a half after sunrise, the convoy came in
from the zeribah. They had been up all night
getting the stores together from the places
where they had been used as parapets, and
loading up the camels, so that they had
had less sleep than we had. I was glad to

find Dickson's wound not so bad as expected,
no artery or bone touched,—a narrow escape,
as the ball went through close to the knee.
Gough also doing well, though he had been
insensible for a long time.

The convoy brought in four men who had
surrendered,—all blacks, who had been in
Hicks's army, and been forced to fight us by
the Arabs. One of them, a sergeant, astonished us by talking very fair Italian. He
was an intelligent man, and gave us a good
lot of news. He was in the Mahdi's dress of
patch-work, and altogether a most comical
fellow to look at. He confessed to having
been one of the men who had fired at us all
night on the 16th and 17th, and said they
had lost many men early on the 17th, when
the Guards and Mounted Infantry went out
to skirmish with them. The gist of the information was, that we had fought Arabs
and regulars from Berber, Arabs from Kordofan, some of the Madhi's troops from Om-

durman, and local levies from Matammeh, with Jalin and Awadiyeh Arabs from the country round—in all, from 9000 to 11,000 men. The enemy's sharpshooters were black soldiers of Hicks's army, and of the garrisons of Obeid and Bara, which had surrendered to the Mahdi, and a few Kordofan hunters. The great charge was delivered by Duguaim, Kenana, and Hamr Arabs from Kordofan, whose contingents with their sheikhs and emirs were almost annihilated. The Jalin and Matammeh men were in reserve, and the Awadiyeh did the cavalry scouting. We were also told that Omdurman had fallen about a fortnight previously,[1] thus setting free many of the Mahdi's troops; and that the force we had defeated was only the advanced-guard of

---

[1] We afterwards ascertained that Omdurman fell only a short time before the Arabs who fought us at Abu Klea left the Mahdi's camp; probably between the 6th and 13th January.

a large army which was expected to reach Matammeh to-day.

Amongst the papers secured were : a copy of prayers composed by the Mahdi, which Sheikh Musa was reading when he broke the square ; a letter from the Mahdi to the governor of Shendy and others, encouraging them to fight the enemies of God, &c. ; and an interesting letter from the Emir of Berber.[1] From the Emir of Berber's letter it is evident that the concentration of Arabs to fight us at Abu Klea took place after, and was consequent upon, Stewart's occupation of Jakdul; so that if he had gone straight across, as at one time intended, he would have met with no opposition in the desert, and probably not much at Matammeh. The original plan had to be given up for want of transport. Another thousand camels, which might have been easily got in November, would have done the business.

[1] Appendix IV.

Gordon's message by his last messenger was
emphatic: "Come by way of Matammeh
or Berber; only by these two roads. Do
this without letting rumours of your approach spread abroad." And here we had
told every one, by our occupation of Jakdul,
that we were moving by the Matammeh
road. Stewart's first march was a complete
surprise. The Arabs did not know of it till
the morning he started; and Omdurman not
having then fallen, the Mahdi could not
have sent down so many troops, even if he
had had time to do so.

The injunction to fight only with spears
and swords is very curious, and confirms
what we had heard of the Mahdi's instructions. Many of the poor fellows who had
obeyed this injunction were mere lads of
sixteen or seventeen. There were also
several letters from Muhammed el Kheir,
Emir of Berber — one about dissensions
amongst the Mahdi's followers—and a lot

of accounts of money expenditure, some of
which were six years old. I could not help
admiring the spirit shown by the two
Arab prisoners we had secured, both badly
wounded. They were quite ready to admit
that they had been badly beaten, but their
faith in the Mahdi, and our eventual de-
struction by him, was as strong as ever.

We were all busy enough during the day
preparing for a move, filling up water-
bottles, and commencing a small fort to
protect the wounded we were obliged to
leave behind, with a detachment of the
Sussex Regiment. At 3.30 P.M. we commenced our march. Just before starting
I went to say good-bye to Dickson and
St Vincent,—the former very low at being
left behind, though otherwise well; the
latter in a troubled sleep, but apparently
in no great pain. Then I went on to catch
up the head of the column.

Stewart's intention was to proceed along

the Matammeh road; and after passing
the wells of Shebacat, and getting within
a few miles of Matammeh, to turn to the
right and strike the Nile about three miles
above the town. This he hoped to do
before daybreak, and then after breakfast
to attack the town. The ordinary guides
we had did not know the country; but
Ali Loda—the robber caught in the desert
—said he knew the country well, and could
take us to the river without going to
Matammeh. He said there were many trees
on the way, and expressed doubts as to our
being able to pass on a dark moonless night.
He was, however, told he must go, and was
promised a good reward if he brought us
down to the Nile all right.

Bearings of the direct route, and of the
road we should have to follow after diverg-
ing from the main track, were taken from
the map, so as to check Ali Loda. Verner
was then given instructions to guide the

column in the required direction, and to use his compass frequently after dark. He did his work well, but from no fault of his the march was not a success. I had always been dubious about the advisability of these night-marches, and before starting spoke to Stewart about this one, and pointed out that the men had had no sleep for two nights.. He was, however, very sanguine; said that the men were in capital spirits, and that as it was only a matter of 25 miles, we should be at the Nile long before daybreak, and in time for the men to have a good rest before fighting.

We moved off from the wells with the Hussars in front, then the Guards, and after them the convoy, Heavies, and Mounted Infantry. At first our way lay down the valley, but suddenly turned to the right over a low spur, whence we had a fine view of the great plain which reaches to the Nile. We got on very well and with

few halts until sunset—the road being level
and well defined, with but little vegetation.
At sunset we had a longer halt for every
one to close up; and about this time we
picked up a poor Arab lad, who, though
badly wounded, had tried to struggle to
the Nile.

· As long as it was daylight I rode with
Stewart, but after sunset I went on to
the head of the column, where Verner
and Stuart-Wortley were with the guides;
and during the remainder of the night I
was either with them, or between them and
the leading company of the Guards (Gordon Cumming's). For the first two hours
we got on very well; for though the night
was dark, the road was good and the pathway quite plain in the starlight, showing
up white in the darkness. Gradually, however, the tall savas grass got thicker, and
the ground broken and rough; the soil was
lighter, and the numerous tracks worn by

D

the camels were really ruts over which the
grass hung. Here the camels, marching on
a broad front but in close order, began to
tumble about; and many were so hungry,
that their riders could hardly prevent their
feeding, and so getting out of their places.
The halts became frequent, to allow the
camels with baggage to close up. After
about two hours of this work, the guides
reported that we were getting near the
wells, and Stewart dismounted the Guards
in case any of the enemy, lurking about,
should attempt an attack.

The trees now began to increase in number, and at last we got into the thicket
of acacia which Ali Loda had described.
The tracks, which had been numerous, began
to diminish in number, until there was only
room for a half-section of cavalry to pass
between the scrub on either side. I was
riding close to the guides at the time, so
had a clear view ahead and few people near

me; yet even then I had some little trouble in avoiding the long sharp thorns of the bushes.

The column got into terrible disorder here. The mounted portion got through fairly enough, but the baggage-camels got jammed and entangled in the bush: many were left behind, others were extricated with difficulty. The confusion was endless, and the noise of swearing men and "grousing" camels could have been heard miles away. The passage through the bush would have been troublesome enough in daylight for a convoy as large as ours; at night, with no moon, it was exceedingly difficult. Halts were frequent, and for a long time we made little progress; but at last we got out on to open ground with gravel, and Ali Loda said we had thence a straight run in to Matammeh.

Here we had a long halt, during which I had a talk with Stewart over the situation.

I was in favour of going along the road to within two or three miles of Matammeh, and then halting to let the men have a good rest before daylight, after which we could attack the town; and I pointed out that men and animals were very tired, and that a long halt on the right road would enable the transport animals to close up and stragglers to come in. Stewart was, however, determined to go on and get to the river without fighting. He was quite opposed to the idea of fighting before reaching the Nile, and thought we should be in a much better position if we fought with our backs to the river, and made sure of water.

About 1 A.M. Verner calculated we had come over fifteen miles, the distance at which we were to turn off; and here the difficulty of marching on a dark night over a country we did not know, and without a track, had to be considered. Ali Loda was called up and questioned. He was very positive

about being able to find his way, and
said we had passed the worst of the grass
and trees. We afterwards found that Ali
had led us well, but was making for a
point higher up the Nile than Stewart
wished.

Stewart decided to go on, and the guide
was told to take us well clear of and out of
sight of Matammeh. A bearing was taken
from the map for Verner to use, and I
picked it up on the stars to keep a check
on both. At 1.15 A.M. we moved on over
a fair country, with scattered trees and no
path. The column, which had become disor-
ganised during its passage through the bush,
seemed now to have got into hopeless confusion; men and animals were quite worn
out, progress was slow, and there were frequent and long halts. I rode with or close
to the guides, and during the halts generally went back to Stewart, who rode near
the leading company of the Guards.

It was a strange experience. During the halts loaded camels, whose drivers had fallen asleep or allowed them to get loose in the dark, kept moving on until they reached the head of the column, and appeared before us gaunt, spectre-like, in the dim starlight. Then, as we moved on they moved, so that at last the head of the column was a mob of guides, hussars, and driverless camels. We tried to get rid of the brutes, but had to give it up as hopeless, for we could get hold of no drivers, and the animals would not be driven back. So great was the confusion, that at one halt part of the column, following some of these loaded camels, came up from near the rear to the front. All this was very wearying for the men, and those marching were rather done up with their struggle through the savas grass and bushes. Directly the halt sounded, every man lay down, to snatch, if he could, a few minutes' sleep.

But the most extraordinary feature was the noise. From the transport animals and their drivers a loud continuous roar rose up to the sky, which must have been easily heard at Matammeh, and probably gave the enemy their first notice of our flank-march.

Progress was very slow—not a mile an hour; and when Venus rose about half an hour before daylight, Stewart determined to halt until we could see where we were, and to allow the rear to close up. According to our calculations we ought then to have been close to the river; but Ali Loda still talked of it as being some distance off, and we began to think he was taking us much too far away from Matammeh, as Stewart did not want to strike the river more than three miles above the town. At any rate, we could not now reach the Nile before daylight, so Stewart sent for Ali Loda, and ordered him to take the shortest cut he could to the river, hoping

that we should get there before we were
observed by the enemy.

Jan. 19th.—When it was light enough
to see the country round, we rose from our
short rest and continued our march, Ali
Loda leading in a direction more to the
left than that which we had been following. This change of direction was .
made by Stewart, who gave Ali his
orders through his own interpreter, and
placed him under a cavalry escort. We
were now about six miles from the Nile,
marching over an open country, with scattered trees, but no sign of the river. Though
it was daylight, we moved slowly, the
camels were so tired; and after we had
gone about two miles a halt was called, and
Verner was sent out to reconnoitre. Here
we came across several herds of goats, which
were promptly annexed, and supplied those
who were in front with a good drink of
milk. We also secured one of the goat-

herds, a black slave, but we were not able to get much out of him.

Again we moved on, and met Verner returning with the report that he had seen Matammeh, with troops in regular formation moving over the gravel ridge on which the town was built ; that he had heard tom-toms going, and seen mounted men moving rapidly along the ridge; and beyond, to the right, the vegetation bordering the Nile. There was no chance now of getting to the Nile without being seen, so we kept on until we got in full sight of Matammeh and the enemy, the Hussars being pushed out as far as it was prudent for their tired horses to go.

It was now about seven, and we could see the enemy moving down to intercept our march to the river. I asked Stewart what he was going to do, and he told me he was going to close up the transport, and then march for the river, with his fighting men

on the left between the transport and Matammeh. I then went out to the hussar
scouts to have a look at the enemy and
the ground in front. As the enemy
advanced and kept working round our
front, I retired, and found all the baggage-
camels packed closely together on an open
gravel place, with the riding-camels round
them, and the fighting men forming an
irregular oblong outside of all. I met
Stewart just outside, and he told me that
he did not think the enemy were coming
on, and that he intended to let the men
have their breakfasts, and then go out and
fight. The camels were so closely packed
that I had some trouble in finding a place
for mine. I got him down, however, at
last, and then began to hunt about for
my servant, and something to eat.

So ended the night - march, which I
cannot think was necessary, for the days
were not hot, and the men would have

fought much better after a night's sleep
and a good breakfast.   Had we halted
when the column came to grief in the
bush, every one would have been fresh
in the morning; we should have had our
fight close outside Matammeh, and been
into it and on the Nile by mid-day.   As it
was, we were in *laager*, with camels and
horses that could scarcely walk, and men
who had been marching all night, and who
had had no rest for three consecutive nights.
Men under such circumstances get into a
nervous "jumpy" state, which might lead
to a grave disaster.

So great was the disorder during the
night, and so dark was it, that a couple of
hundred men knowing the ground might
have given us serious trouble; and we owed
our safety as much as anything to the
inactivity of the enemy.   —— told me he
had found it quite impossible to keep the
animals together during the night.   Most

of the drivers were Aden boys, not knowing
English; so you may imagine the difficulty
of controlling them on a dark night in a
wooded country. No one will ever know
the number of camels lost during the march,
but it is supposed that over 100 disappeared
with their loads.

—— worked hard all night; he was
never still for a moment, and when day
broke, he was so done up that each camel
looked like two. He had been in the
fight of the 17th near the bad corner where
the square broke; had then marched back
from the wells to the zeribah, and been up
all night working hard at the stores,—so
that he had been on the go without sleep
for over forty-eight hours. A short rest
and some food soon set him right, and he
was well to the front afterwards.

I had scarcely settled down to eat something when bullets began to whistle overhead. The enemy ran round our front with

great rapidity, and soon began firing upon us from the long grass on the right and left. By 8 A.M. they had got well round us, and bullets began to drop pretty freely into the square. Stewart then ordered the formation of a zeribah of camel-saddles and commissariat-boxes to protect the men. No one now thought of breakfast, and I fear many of the men got nothing to eat, and water was not at all plentiful.

By degrees the enemy worked all round us, and their fire got unpleasant; men were hit here and there, and the hospital began to fill up.

The rough sketch will show something of the position. At 1 the Hussars came in, and after picketing their horses, formed up in front of them; next came the R.E., who were out cutting brushwood for the zeribah; then the sadly reduced Naval Brigade, under Beresford; and after them in succession the Artillery and Mounted

Infantry, the Guards, the Heavies, and the
Sussex Regiment.   In the centre were the
camels; and at 8—the highest point of

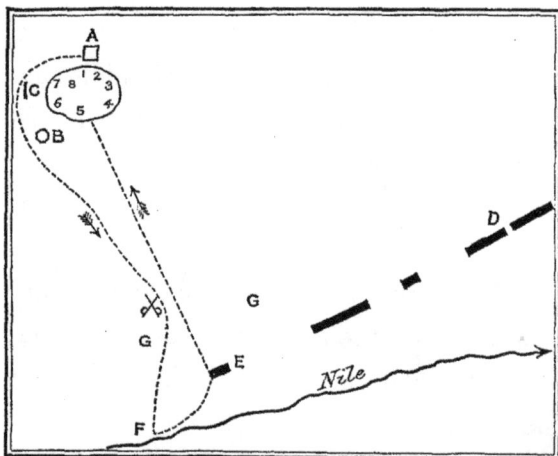

1, Hussars; 2, R.E. Det.; 3, Navy and Gardner gun; 4,
Mounted Infantry and Artillery; 5, Guards; 6, Heavies; 7,
Sussex; 8, Hospital. *A*, Place where square was formed up; *B*,
Knoll and small redoubt; *C*, Trench for dead; *D*, Matammeh;
E, Gubat; *F*, Where we struck river; - - - - - - - Route of square;
G, Slope from which the spearmen charged.

what might be called a gravel island in a
sea of savas grass—was the hospital.   At *B*,
about 40 yards off, there was a small gravel

knoll, rather higher than that on which the square was ; and then, all round, grass and bushes in which the enemy were concealed. We never saw them, and could only judge of their position by the puffs of smoke. *A* is the point where the square was formed up to march to the Nile, and *C* the trench where the dead were buried next day ; *D*, Matammeh, from 2 to 2½ miles distant ; *E*, Gubat ; and *F*, the point where we struck the river and bivouacked. *G* is the gravel ridge from which the spearmen charged down upon us.

As the fire became hotter the parapet in front of the men grew in height, and here and there traverses of boxes were built up as a protection against the enfilading fire. A few men were also sent out to the knoll *B*, to prevent its occupation by the enemy; but otherwise nothing was done. About 10.15 A.M. Stewart was wounded, and carried to the hospital. The command then devolved upon me as senior officer. After a short talk with Boscawen, who was next senior officer, we went together to Stewart, and found him very cool and collected, and apparently not in great pain; but on my saying I hoped he would soon be well, he at once replied that he was certain the wound was fatal, and that his soldiering days were over. I said what I could to cheer him; but time was passing, and as I did not wish to disturb him more than was necessary, I asked what he had intended doing if he had not been hit. He said he thought the best thing to be done was to go straight at Matammeh or to repeat the Abu Klea plan of going out to fight for the water, and then returning to the zeribah to carry the wounded, stores, &c., down to the Nile.

At this time it was quite evident that the enemy had received their expected reinforcements from Omdurman, including regular soldiers, and that we had a large force in front of us. We could see lines of banners on our left, front, and right; and things were beginning to look rather unpleasant. I told Stewart that I should go out and fight as soon as I could, and if circumstances were favourable, try Matammeh. I then went off to arrange details with Boscawen. Stewart was very tenderly nursed by Rhodes, his A.D.C., and St Leger Herbert, until the latter was killed; and his wound was much regretted by every one, for he was deservedly very popular with officers and men, and no one could help admiring his fearlessness in the midst of danger.

The enemy's fire on the front and right having become rather warm, two companies, one from the Guards and one from the Mounted Infantry, were sent out as skirmishers to keep it down. The organisation of the square was next settled: it was

E

formed, somewhat as at Abu Klea, with the
Guards and Mounted Infantry in front, and
the Heavies and Sussex in rear; but half
the Heavies, and the Royal Artillery and
Naval Brigade with their guns and Gardner, were left in the zeribah, and only the
camels absolutely necessary for the cacolets,
reserve ammunition, and water, were taken.
At each angle there were small reserves, dismounted hussars and sappers, to meet a
sudden rush.

Before marching for the Nile, it was
necessary to leave the zeribah in a condition
to resist any attack that might be made
upon it after the square had left; and two
small redoubts, both constructed of commissariat stores and camel - saddles, were
commenced—one on the knoll *B*, the other
at No. 8, to protect the hospital. Shortly
after the skirmishers had gone out, a small
breastwork of boxes was erected to protect
the men lying down on the knoll *B*. It

was a troublesome piece of work, as the boxes had to be carried for about forty yards under fire; and the first were taken across by volunteers, amongst whom was Mr Burleigh, the 'Daily Telegraph' correspondent.

When it was decided to turn the breastwork into a redoubt, the officers and men of the Heavies and Guards worked in a splendid way, all joining in carrying the boxes out. Lawson, with some of the sappers, was hard at work, and so was ———, in spite of his fatigue of the previous night; all the officers were equally active. The construction of the redoubt to protect the hospital, which was "engineered" by Dorward, was nearly as dangerous, for bullets were now flying about in all directions. It was hard work, for the boxes had to be carried inwards from the parapet which had been made in front of the zeribah; and this had to be done by passing between camels

packed so closely together that there was
scarcely room to move about. It was this
difficulty of getting about amidst the crowded camels that caused so many delays, and
it was quite 2 P.M. before the units of the
square began to disentangle themselves after
leaving the two redoubts in a state in which
they could be completed by the garrisons to
be left in them.

During this time there were many casualties. Cameron of the 'Standard' was
shot early. He had had a presentiment of
his coming end, and during the night-march
had been full of forebodings. He had seated
himself near his camels, and was shot as he
had half risen to get a box of sardines from
his servant.

St Leger Herbert was shot through the
head as he was going to get his water-bottle
before joining the square, and death must
have been instantaneous. I had only seen
him a few moments before writing from

Stewart's dictation, when I went to say
"good-bye" before joining the square.

Crutchley, adjutant of the Guards, was
badly hit in the leg as he was talking to
Dorward, who, true to his R.E. training,
was bothering him for a receipt for some
intrenching tools.

Whilst the square was forming the enemy
kept up a heavy fire, which was well replied
to from the two redoubts; and as each
corps came up, it lay down on the ground
in proper position. The place selected for
assembly was just outside the Hussars, as
the fire was less heavy on that side than the
others. During the time of preparation I
was constantly moving about to see all that
was going on, and could not help noticing,
and feeling for, the wretched camels tied
tightly down in the zeribah. The most curious thing was that they showed no alarm,
and did not seem to mind being hit. One
heard a heavy thud, and looking round, saw

a stream of blood oozing out of the wound, but the camel went on chewing his cud as if nothing at all had happened, not even giving a slight wince to show he was in pain.

The garrison left in the zeribah consisted of the 19th Hussars, whose horses were so worn out they could not act as cavalry, and could barely carry their riders; the R.A. with their guns, under Norton and Du Boulay; half the R.E., under Dorward; the Naval Brigade, under Beresford; and half the Heavy Camels, under Davison of the 16th Lancers. I left Barrow in command of the force under Lord C. Beresford, who was senior officer in rank, and the small redoubt on the knoll was occupied by some of the Heavies. The square was made up of one-half the Heavies, under Talbot; the Guards, under Willson; the Mounted Infantry, under the younger Barrow; the Sussex, under Sunderland; R.E. with Lawson; and a few dismounted 19th Hussars, under Craven.

All the correspondents remained in the zeribah, except Villiers of the 'Graphic.' I think there were some doubts about our getting through to the Nile, for by this time the gravel terrace in front of us was swarming with foot and horse, and in front of them their banners fluttered gaily in the breeze. We all realised that we had our work cut out for us; and many felt that if we did not reach water that night, it would go hard with the whole force.

I fully felt the gravity of the situation, but from the moment I entered the square I felt no anxiety as to the result. The men's faces were set in a determined way which meant business, and I knew they intended to drink from the Nile that night. I was never so much struck with the appearance of the men; they moved in a cool, collected way, without noise or any appear-

ance of excitement. Many, as I afterwards
heard, never expected to get through, but
were determined to sell their lives dearly.
One officer's servant came with a large skin
of water, determined, as he afterwards said,
not to die thirsty.

When I got into the square I asked Boscawen to take executive command, and move
off round the small redoubt *B* to the river,
and told Verner to give the square its direction. Directly the men rose from the
ground the enemy opened fire, and as we
were moving round the redoubt, we got well
into the line of fire. Several men dropped
at once, and we began to think we were
going to have a bad time of it. We here
quickened our pace, leaving the wounded on
the ground to be carried back to the zeribah,
which was only 25 or 30 yards distant.
They were all got in, and I hear the
Heavies in the redoubt were very active
in giving assistance.

When we got clear of the redoubt, we
made for a gravel ridge on which a large
force of the enemy was collected with their
banners, and behind which we knew lay the
Nile. We did not go straight, but zigzag,
to keep as much as possible on the bare
gravel patches, over which men and camels
could march more freely than through the
savas grass; and we went at a sauntering
pace in consequence of the camels in the
square.

The enemy's sharpshooters, who were well
concealed in the long grass, and behind and
beneath the trees and bushes, kept up a continuous fire on the square during its march.
We could not send out skirmishers to reply to
them, for fear of a sudden rush of spearmen as
at Abu Klea; and the ground was much more
dangerous, and likely to conceal large bodies
of men, than that of the Abu Klea valley.
All we could do was, when we got into a
warm spot, to lie down and fire volleys at

the puffs of smoke in the long grass; then,
when we had checked the fire a little, to
rise and move on. It was curious to notice
the degrees of intensity of fire we passed
through. For a few minutes we would go
on with nothing more than the weird
soughing of the bullets overhead; then we
would get to a spot where the bullets
whistled sharp and clear, and occasional
thuds told they had found a home.

One of the first to be hit was my native
interpreter, Muhammed Effendi Ibrahim,
who had behaved in a most plucky way at
Abu Klea. Luckily it was only a flesh-
wound in the side, and he was soon hoisted
on a camel, where he solaced himself with
a cigarette, and surveyed the surrounding
scene. His was a curious history. He was
a friend of Arabi Pasha, and after Tel-el-
Kebir escaped to Sheikh Senusi, in the
desert south of Tripoli. After the amnesty,
he returned to Cairo, and entered the secret

police; he left them for some fancied slight
from the English commandant, and became
Webber's interpreter; then I heard of him,
and secured his services.   He was most use-
ful at Dongola, as, being a Moslem, he could
mix with the people and find out what was
going on.

Later in the afternoon Lord Arthur
Somerset was struck over the heart by a
spent ball.   He thought he was mortally
wounded, but luckily, though the shock
was great, the ball did not penetrate.
There was, however, a dreadful bruise; and
his chest was made so tender that he caught
cold during the bivouac, and got congestion
of the lungs and all sorts of complications
afterwards.   He also had a slight wound in
the left arm, which had to be put in a sling.
Count Gleichen was also hit; but the bullet
turned, on some trinket I think, and he was
not wounded.

What with halts to fire, and a zigzag

course, our progress was slow, and the sun
was getting low when we got within about
600 yards of the ridge.   Here we got into
a very hot place : seven men were shot dead,
and men fell so quickly that the cacolets
and stretchers were filled.   Things began to
look ugly, and some of the officers told me
afterwards that they thought we should
have been obliged to turn back without
reaching the Nile.   That, however, we should
never have done, as failure meant anni-
hilation.   I was walking just behind the
Marines, and one poor fellow fell dead
almost into my arms.   The men were quite
steady, with a set, determined look about
their faces, and I knew they could be
trusted.

All at once, as suddenly as at Abu Klea,
the firing ceased, and the enemy's spearmen
came running down the hill at a great pace,
with several horsemen in front.   It was a
relief to know the crisis had come.   The

square was at once halted to receive the
charge, and the men gave vent to their
feelings in a wild spontaneous cheer.   Then
they set to work, firing as they would have
done at an Aldershot field-day.   At first
the fire had little effect, and the bugle
sounded " cease firing "—the men, much
to my surprise, answering to the call.   The
momentary rest steadied them, and when
the enemy got within about 300 yards, they
responded to the call " commence firing "
with deadly effect.   All the leaders with
their fluttering banners went down, and
no one got within 50 yards of the square.
It only lasted a few minutes : the whole of
the front ranks were swept away ; and then
we saw a backward movement, followed by
the rapid disappearance of the Arabs in
front of and all round us.

We had won, and gave three ringing
cheers ; but we had still to reach the Nile
with our heavy train of wounded, and men

weary with constant excitement and want
of sleep. I received the congratulations of
Boscawen and several other officers, and
thanked and complimented Boscawen in
return for the way in which he had
handled the square. The number of the
enemy on the gravel hills and round us—
that is to say, on the field of battle—was,
I should think, very nearly as great as
at Abu Klea; but the number of spearmen
who charged was only about 800, as against
about 1500 at Abu Klea. They charged
in the same formation — a sort of triple
phalanx—and with the same determination;
and running down-hill, came with greater
impetus; but the superior steadiness of
the men, and their more accurate fire
on this occasion, never gave them a
chance. They left all their leaders and
from 250 to 300 dead in front of the
square; but we found out afterwards that
many more had been killed in the long

grass and behind the ridge, and that a large number of wounded had been taken off to Matammeh.

During our march the garrison in the zeribah had been engaged with the enemy's riflemen at long ranges, but they never came to close quarters; and the guns had been firing away cheerily at the dense masses of the enemy on the gravel hills in front of the square. As we marched along we could see some of the shells bursting and scattering the crowds; and I think it was chiefly owing to the accuracy of the artillery-fire that a larger number of spearmen did not charge us.

The square was halted for a few minutes after the fight was over, to fill up pouches with ammunition, and let the men have a good drink of water; then we moved on, glad to think that we had not lost a single man by this last charge, and that, a remarkable exception to all previous fights in the

Sudan, no one had been touched by sword or spear.

By the time we had reached the top of the gravel ridge the sun was just disappearing, and we were terribly disappointed not to see the Nile, which we had hoped would have been close in front of us. We could see, however, the line of green vegetation and the houses of the villages. We knew the Nile must be there, but it seemed a long way off to weary men. At first we moved towards a small village ; but as night came on, thought it better to move a little to the right, and strike the river where there were no houses, and no chance of encountering an enemy. We went down a shallow ravine, at the end of which there was a belt of cultivation and vegetation, peas, mimosa, and some dura.

Wortley, I, and a few others left the square at the head of the ravine, and went down to select a camping-place. Consider-

ing we had to look for one after dark, we
were pretty successful; and we had what
we had often longed for during the day—
an unstinted drink of water. The square
got in about half an hour after dark, and
the wounded were at once taken to the best
place we could find on the bank of the
river; the men went down to drink by companies; and the camels were turned into the
pea-fields. Directly every one had had a
drink, I sent Lawson away with his sappers
to cut bush for a zeribah, and had pickets
posted on each side of the ravine we had
come down.

The men were so exhausted that when
they came up from their drink at the river
they fell down like logs, and we had some
trouble in rousing them and getting them
into their places for the night. We found
very few of them had brought rations or
anything to eat: with 150 rounds of rifle-

F

ammunition, they preferred leaving their
food behind to carrying the extra weight.
Wortley's servant had brought a tin of Chi-
cago beef and some biscuit, upon which
we supped, and were able to share it with
Cumming, Romilly, and Bonham, who had
brought little with them.

Before lying down, I went to see the
wounded, who were having their wounds
dressed. The doctors behaved splendidly;
nothing could have been better. They had
been up three nights and through two
fights, and here they were again working
on the fourth night. One of them, I believe, fainted from exhaustion, but they
went on until every wounded man had
been attended. The bearer-company also
behaved admirably: not a wounded man
was left on the ground; every one was at
once picked up and put into a cacolet on
a camel or on to a stretcher. The hospital
after a fight is a horrible sight, but the men

bore their wounds nobly, and were much quieter than I expected.

After the hospital, I went round the zeribah, and then lay down to sleep. I had sent my second interpreter for my ulster, and only in the evening found he had not got it—said he could not find my camel; I expect he was too frightened to look for it. Wortley had managed to bring the Abu Klea carpet and a coat; so Verner and I slept under the former, and he in his own coat. I slept very soundly at first, but as the night wore on it got bitterly cold, and one could only sleep by snatches.

We were all thankful to have reached the Nile and secured water, though in a somewhat crippled state, and we knew not what the morrow would bring forth. Every one behaved well; and it would be impossible to speak too highly of the steadiness of the Guards and Mounted Infantry, who

were in the face of the square against which
the enemy directed their charge.   There
was no opening for special acts of bravery,
and it would be almost unfair to partic-
ularise any corps or regiment.   Throughout
the fight there was a marked absence of
that super-excitement which struck me so
much when, for a few moments, some of
the men got " out of hand " at Abu Klea.

Jan. 20th.—We were up by daylight,
and at once began preparations for moving
the zeribah down.   The first thing was to
fill up all the water-skins and tanks we
had, for we knew they had nothing but the
muddy water from Abu Klea.   Then, as
soon as it was light enough, small scouting-
parties were sent up and down the river.
The first returned with a black slave, who
had given himself up, and who reported no
enemy in that direction.   The second party
soon sent back to say there was no one
in an old building we had noticed down-

stream, and that the nearest village appeared to be deserted.

The Heavies were then left under Colonel Talbot as a guard for the wounded, and I moved on with the Guards and Mounted Infantry to occupy the village. It was quite empty, and situated on a gravel terrace overlooking the Nile, and about three-quarters of a mile from it. The place was Abu Kru, but somehow or other it got to be called Gubat. The wounded were now brought up, and Lawson and his sappers were set to work to place the houses in a state of defence. After the wounded were fairly settled, a small garrison of Sussex and Heavies was left to protect them, and we formed up outside to march back to the zeribah.

I had been a little anxious about the zeribah, not knowing what had happened there. As far as we could judge from our glasses, it was all right; but crowds of the

enemy were hanging about, and we could
see two of our riding - camels with their
bright red saddles being led into Matammeh.   Whether they had been taken from
the zeribah or were lost on the night-march,
we did not know. As we were moving off,
the enemy assembled in large numbers on
the gravel hill close to Matammeh, and we
fully expected an attack. The men, though
they had had no food, were in good heart,
and freshened by their night's rest, so
we determined to offer battle. When they
saw we were ready for another fight, they
began to disperse; and some volleys at long
range, which killed a few men, hastened
their movements.   We then resumed our
march to the zeribah, leaving the battle-field
of yesterday to our left, and reached it
without further opposition.

The garrison received us with hearty
cheers, which I think were more grateful to
us than any after-rewards will be.   We felt

that under trying circumstances we had done our duty like men, and that the lusty cheers were the spontaneous vote of thanks of our comrades for having pulled ourselves and them out of an awkward position. I was congratulated by Barrow, Beresford, and others, and after giving orders for a move down to the river, went to see Stewart. I found he had passed a fairly good night, and was not quite so low about himself. The doctors, too, gave a favourable account of his symptoms, and he had not much pain except when moving.

The zeribah was in a state of much confusion,[1] and presented a strange sight. The number of wounded was so large that they had been obliged to increase the size of the little fort, and use up ammunition,

[1] This refers to the way in which the commissariat stores, saddles, &c., were mixed up in the breastwork. The two redoubts had been much strengthened during the absence of the square ; and everything connected with the defence and the garrison was in perfect order.

commissariat, and all kinds of boxes, not to mention the camel - saddles, for its walls. It seemed at first hopeless to get things into shape again. It was wretched to see the number of dead and wounded camels and horses. The former, especially, had suffered severely, having been packed so closely together.

The enemy's riflemen had kept up their fire on the zeribah, but not so hotly, until the spearmen were defeated by the square; then they retired, and the men had a quiet night, which I am sorry to say was given up to looting the stores in the zeribah. The native drivers, boys from Aden, were the worst, and some of the ——, who attacked the medical comforts, brandy, champagne, &c., for the sick and wounded —the worst kind of robbery. When visiting the wounded, I found one of these wretched men, who should have been nursing his bleeding comrades, hopelessly and

noisily drunk. I was very wroth, and
longed for a return of the days when a
man could be triced up and given four
dozen lashes. All I could do was to have
the brute tied up to a tree in the sun. I
was very unfortunate in having the most
stupid of servants. My ulster was taken,
and all my small supply of stores, cocoa
and milk, compressed tea, &c., was looted
—the box broken open, and nothing left
but a few sheets of foolscap. The men
who had been left in the zeribah began getting the stores together at once, and as soon
as we had had our breakfast we joined them.
Barrow went on directly he could get away,
as his horses were quite done up from want
of water ; and we sent with him some food
for the men who had been left at Abu Kru.

The work of pulling down the zeribah
walls of boxes and saddles, getting the
camels out of the crowded pen in which
they were, saddling and loading them up,

was very heavy and trying for the men ;
but they worked with a will, and things
began to get into shape.   Stewart's little
shelter was left to the last, so as to expose
him to the sun as little ·as possible.   We
found as we went on that the losses in
camels had been so large, and those that
remained were so weak, that we could not
carry all the stores down at one journey ; so
we had to leave the small redoubt *B* with
a larger garrison than before, and make it
as strong as possible—so strong that it
could not be rushed.   ·

About mid-day we buried the dead.
Beresford asked if he might read the service, to which I consented, and I attended
as chief mourner.   Poor St Leger Herbert,
what a bright young life to be cut off so
soon !   He was a most amusing companion,
and a man of brilliant talents, who, if he had
been spared, would have made his mark in
the world.   The work of dismantling the

zeribah was at last finished, and all the
wounded carried out to their place in the
column; then we marched for Abu Kru.
Before leaving I took a last turn round,
saw the little redoubt was quite safe, and
told Davison, who was left in command,
to collect all the *débris* lying about, and
burn it before he left next day, so that
the enemy might not know how much we
had suffered.

As we passed the battle-field, Pöe of the
Marines was sent out to bury our dead, and
I went with him to see if they had been
mutilated, and whether any of them had
been alive when left behind. I was relieved
to find that all of them had bullet-wounds
which must have caused immediate death;
and though the bodies had been stripped,
and three of them had been much cut about
with spears and swords, there was none of
that mutilation which is such a horrid
feature in fights with some savages. Dur-

ing the night the Arabs had buried their
principal men, but I counted over 200
bodies still lying on the ground; they all
had the Mahdi's uniform, and the string of
ninety-nine beads round their necks. Some
of them were fine men, Arabs from Kordofan, like those who fought at Abu Klea;
whilst others were black regulars, and a few
were Jalin from the neighbourhood. We
found two or three wounded, whom we carried on with us. From these men we had
confirmation of the fall of Omdurman, and
heard that another force under Feki Mustafa was on its way from Khartum to fight
us, and that one was also coming up the
river from Berber; so we had every prospect
of more fighting.

The march of the column was very slow,
owing to the wounded, who must have
suffered greatly; but they bore it well,
and before sunset all were under cover at
Abu Kru. Stewart stood the shaking

much better than we expected, and every one hoped his would not prove a bad case. We found all right in the village, which had been turned into a strong post; but unfortunately many of the rush huts and roofs had been burned,—some had been fired without orders in the morning, and others later on to clear the ground. Before dark the troops got into position for bivouac,—Guards in front of the village, the Heavies on left, Mounted Infantry on right, and Hussars and camels on the ground between the village and the river. In the village were the Sussex Regiment, the wounded, and the Commissariat.

We had now secured ourselves on the Nile, and this is the place to consider the state in which we got there. First as regards the men. They had had no proper sleep on the night of the 16th-17th. On

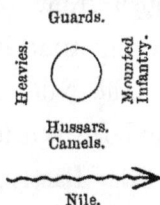

the 17th they had been roughly handled by the enemy, and fully realised they had had a narrow escape.   On the night of the 17th-18th no sleep, and many of them employed all night on fatigue-duty, moving and loading up stores at the zeribah. On the 18th filling up tanks and water-skins at the wells; then the weary night-march through the thick grass and mimosa-bush from 3 P.M. to 7 A.M.   After this the trying time in the zeribah, and the march to the Nile, with its fight,[1] followed by a bivouac without blankets, and with little food.   Lastly, the march back to the zeribah on the 20th, with the heavy work of dismantling the zeribah, loading up the camels, and carrying the wounded down.   It may be said that the men arrived at the Nile after four days of exceptional exertion under a tropical sun, without having had one night's

---

[1] On the 19th the men were under fire from about 8 A.M. till 5 P.M.—about nine hours.

rest, and after having lost, in killed and
wounded, more than one-tenth of their number. They were in capital spirits, and the
complete success of the previous day's fight
had quite restored their confidence in themselves, which had been a little shaken at
Abu Klea. Still they needed rest; and
we knew no reinforcements were going to
be sent or would start until we could get
a message through to Lord Wolseley.

Next as regards the camels. They had
been watered on the 13th and 14th, and
did not get water again until the 19th and
20th. They had therefore been without
water for from six to seven days, having
previously been accustomed to water every
second or third day. The camels started
from Jakdul with about 12 lb. of dura each,
or 3 lb. a-day for four days, the usual allowance being 9 lb. They were thus on
one-third rations, which they did not always get, for four days only out of six.

From 2 P.M. on the 16th to 3 A.M. on the
18th, some thirty-seven hours, they were
tied down so tightly in the zeribah, before
Abu Klea, that they could not move a limb,
and I doubt if they were fed at all during
that time.   Then from 3 P.M. on 18th to
7 A.M. on 19th, or sixteen hours, they were
on the march, part of the time struggling
through savas grass and mimosa by night;
and they probably had their loads on for
seventeen or eighteen hours.   This was
followed by another tying down in a zeribah
for over twenty-four hours without any
food.   Can it be wondered at that the poor
beasts were hardly able to crawl down to
the river with their loads, and that they
were practically useless without some rest
and food ?   The result almost justified the
mot, that we thought we had found in the
camel an animal that required neither food,
drink, nor rest : we certainly acted as if the
camel were a piece of machinery.   The sore

backs from careless loading in the dark, and from tumbling about during the night-marches, were sickening to look at.

The cavalry horses were also quite done up. The way in which Barrow managed to bring the 19th Hussars across the desert is one of the best things in the expedition; but the horses had only had a short drink at Abu Klea, and then they had barely enough to wash their mouths out until they got to the Nile on the 20th. The scouting of the Hussars during the march was admirably done; they were ubiquitous. But want of food and water no horses can fight against, and they were but a sorry spectacle as they moved out of the zeribah to go down to the river. They reached the Nile almost useless as cavalry, and could only be employed for scouting purposes, at short distances from the camp.

Under these circumstances it became a question whether we should be content with

G

our position or attack Matammeh. Some, I
believe, thought we were not strong enough
to attack, and that with 100 wounded we
should not run the risk of largely increasing
the number. I thought over the whole
question, and considered that the political
effect of not taking Matammeh would be so
bad that its capture ought to be attempted.
Besides, as we had seen no signs of the
approach of the expected reinforcements to
the enemy, I hoped we might be able to
take and establish ourselves in the town
before they arrived. I had heard that
on the north side of the town, and near
its centre, there was a large government
building; and I determined if possible to
attack this, feeling sure that if it were
once secured the place would be ours. Arrangements were made to attack as soon
after daybreak as possible, and we then
lay down to sleep.

    Jan. 21*st*.—Last night we had a fire-alarm. The dry thatched roof of one of the houses caught fire, and flared up in grand style; but Pöe, who commanded the fire-picket, was equal to the occasion, and worked hard with his men. I was a little anxious at first, as there was so much ammunition about; but the rafters were soon pulled down, and as there was little wind, the fire was confined to the four mud walls. Luckily the fire was early in the evening, so we got a good sleep afterwards. At the first glimmer of dawn we were on parade, formed up. Barrow with his Hussars started first, taking with him one of the slaves we had picked up, who was to be sent into the village with a letter, calling upon the people to surrender without fighting, and promising them that they would not be molested if they did. Then we advanced in double column, with the guns, and the camels with ammunition, cacolets, and water between the two columns. In this

way we moved much quicker than we had
done in square.

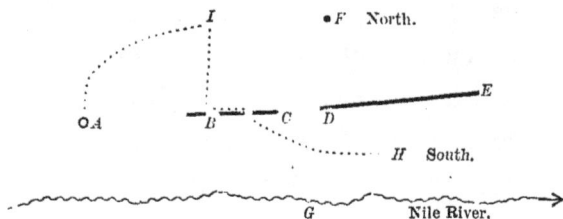

A, Abu Kru ; *B*, Large village ; *C*, House held by R.E. and
M.I ; *D E*, Matammeh ; *D*, Battery ; *F*, Hussars ; *G*, Place where
Gordon's men landed ; *H*, Farthest point of square.

The force consisted of Guards, Heavies,
Mounted Infantry, Naval Brigade with
Gardner, R.A. with guns, R.E., and the
bearer-company.

A little before eight, Barrow sent in to
say that the enemy's cavalry, about 50, had
at first advanced, and then retired before
his volleys to the north-east, over the hills
Our force was then at *I*, and we could see
a row of banners at *D*, and that the village
had no regular openings in its mud walls.
The force was now halted, and I went

out to Barrow and his Hussars at F to reconnoitre.   When I got there I found him
in a capital position on some gravel swell-
ings of ground which quite commanded the
town, and from whence artillery-fire would
take the trench at D, with its defenders, in
reverse.

I had made up my mind to move the
force to the north and attack from these
hills, and was on my way back to give the
orders, when, to my great surprise, I saw
the troops moving off towards B, and one
of the companies open fire.   On the way
back I met ——, who had been sent by
Boscawen with a message to say that he
had seen a body of dervishes moving between the force and the Nile in the direction
of our camp, and that he had moved to the
right to intercept them, as the camp could
not stand a rush.   I caught up the force
at the village B, which was deserted ;
thence I could see no dervishes on the low

ground towards the river, but I was told
that they had been there, and that they
were probably still concealed in the dura,
cotton-bushes, &c., on the plain.

From the village we could see the plain
down to the river covered with cotton-
bushes and a few clumps of trees; and as
there was a possibility of men passing unseen between us and the river to attack the
camp, the force was marched southwards.
We passed between the large village *B,* and
the smaller one *C,* and marched in the
direction of *H.* The Sappers and a company of Mounted Infantry were sent to
occupy the house at *C* nearest to Matammeh, and told to put it in a state of defence.

The enemy had hitherto made no sign;
but about this time Mr Burleigh, the 'Daily
Telegraph' correspondent, riding towards
D, drew their fire. As we went on, now
in square in case of a sudden rush of
spearmen, the enemy opened a brisk fire

from behind loopholed walls, whence we
could see puffs of smoke issuing.   Occasionally the square halted, and the men lay
down whilst skirmishers were sent out to
reply to the fire of the enemy; and we
tried our guns, but they produced no effect
on the mud walls.

Whilst this was going on, and at about
9.30, an orderly came down from Barrow
to say that he could see some large flags in
our rear, and that he was nearly certain
they were on steamers.   Shortly afterwards
we could see them coming down.   Mr Burleigh rode off to meet them, and I sent
Stuart-Wortley to communicate with them,
and arrange with the commander to land
some of his men and take part in the
attack.

We had now been exchanging shots with
the enemy for some time without result,
and at last commenced to withdraw and
move up again to the village B, where

Gordon's men were to join us, as it was
plain the town could not be taken from
the south without very heavy loss. As we
commenced withdrawing, a gun opened upon
us from a battery near D, firing blind-shell;
luckily only one shell came into the square.
I heard the rush of the shot through the air,
and then a heavy thud behind me. I
thought at first it had gone into the field-
hospital, but on looking round found it
had carried away the lower jaw of one of
the artillery camels, and then buried itself
in the ground. The poor brute walked on
as if nothing had happened, and carried its
load to the end of the day.

We had been much elated by the sight
of the steamers, with their large Egyptian
flags, coming down the river; their sudden
appearance had quite a stage effect. We
effected a junction with the troops from the
steamers just below the village; and here I
first made acquaintance with Khashm el

Mus, Abd ul Hamid, and others of Gordon's
army.   The men seemed in high spirits, and
were cordially welcomed by Tommy Atkins.
Only blacks came up, as the Egyptian
Pasha with his fellahin preferred to remain
on board.   The blacks were most amusing
—just like children.   I sent them on to the
front with the guns they had landed, to open
fire on the end *D* of the village, where I
now proposed to attack.   They were soon
firing away merrily from behind the houses
at *C* and the ground to the left.   Whilst
they were advancing I had a long talk with
Khashm el Mus and Abd ul Hamid, and
was shown Gordon's note of 29th December
—" Khartoum all right, and can hold out for
years,"—which they had given to Verner,
who had met the steamers at the camp and
come down with them.   Khashm el Mus
also told me that on their way down they
had seen the force under Feki Mustafa
coming from Khartum, and that it would

reach Gubat in the evening or early next
morning.

Our position now was this : A detachment in a small redoubt at the old zeribah
three miles away ; 100 wounded at Gubat,
with insufficient protection for them and
the stores ; the main body in action before Matammeh, and a force said to be
coming down upon us from the south.
I sent a warning back to camp, and told
them to send up at once for Davison and
the men and stores left at the old zeribah. I then went on to the front to see
how things were getting on, and whether
the guns had been able to make a breach
in the wall. I found they had produced
little effect, the shot simply passing through
the mud walls, and that our own guns had
little ammunition, and no sufficient reserve
in camp to go on firing and leave enough
for the fight we might expect with Feki
Mustafa during the next twenty-four hours.

I now had a consultation with Boscawen,
and as a result, very reluctantly gave the
order to commence retiring on the camp.
It is a fair question for argument whether
we ought to have attacked. In favour was
the moral effect of the capture of the town
on our own men and the enemy, and that
is all. Against it were: We could not
have held the town when taken, as it
was too large for the force, weakened as
it would be by the departure of the convoy and escort, to hold. We could not
have destroyed the mud houses in any
reasonable time. If successful, the losses
would certainly have been heavy, and we
could ill afford them with the prospect of
a fight in the next twenty-four hours. A
repulse, or even a severe check, would have
been disastrous. We had lost one-tenth
of our effective strength, and had 100
wounded in hospital, so that any further
loss in wounded would have seriously ham-

pered and almost crippled us. Besides this, the men were hardly recovered from the exertions of the four previous days; and the organisation of the Camel Corps was not the best that could have been devised for the attack of a town with loopholed walls.

It was a short time before we commenced retiring that Pöe of the Marines was hit in the thigh, a dreadful wound, necessitating amputation very high up. Ever since leaving Korti he had worn a red coat, almost the only one in the force; and I fear this made him too conspicuous. He was shot whilst standing up alone in the open, talking to his men, who were lying down. He was only 400 or 500 yards from the town, and I fear his red coat attracted the attention of the enemy, and brought down upon him a shower of bullets. Boscawen managed the withdrawal cleverly and well; no confusion or hurry, and always giving the enemy a chance to attack us if they wished.

They never, however, ventured out to annoy us. We thus withdrew without pressing the attack home, and did 'nothing more than reconnoitre the town in force; but the moral effect was bad, as we went out intending to attack, and our withdrawal gave the enemy fresh heart.

I think if we had gone at the place at once instead of marching round it to the south, we should have succeeded with the loss of 50 or 60 men. We had, however, established ourselves on the Nile, and that was the main point. On our way back to camp we burned the houses and villages which lay between us and Matammeh, to prevent their being used by the enemy. When I returned to camp between three and four, I found they had made preparations for moving the wounded down to the river, and were waiting orders to do so. There was some excitement about the expected attack, and —— was much excited,

declaring the position a bad one, too far
from the water for the thirsty British
soldier, &c.

I was at first averse to moving the
wounded to a place where they would have
no shade except such as tents could give;
but after talking to Stewart, and finding that
he thought it the best plan, I gave the necessary orders.   Whilst the move was being
made, I opened and read the letters which
Gordon had sent down at various times, the
last lot having been forwarded on the 14th
December by the 'Bordein,' the last steamer
to leave Khartum : this mail, with the last
volume of the 'Journal,' had been intrusted
to a Greek.   The first two letters I opened
were addressed to the officer commanding
her Majesty's troops : one was an order
to Nashi Pasha, the Egyptian commanding the four steamers, to deliver them
over to the English ; the other,[1] a most

[1] Appendix VII.

characteristic letter, telling us to remove all
Egyptians, whether pashas, beys, or privates
—"those hens," he called them—and not
to allow one of them to go up to Khartum
again.   In other letters he wrote in strong
terms of the uselessness and cowardice of
these men, and begged that if the steamers
were not manned by British sailors, they
should return to him with none but Sudanese soldiers and sailors.   These letters were
dated in October, when he first sent the
steamers down to await our arrival, which
he then expected weekly.   I next opened
two letters from Gordon to Lord Wolseley,
which did not give much news ; and at last
opened one to Watson, knowing Gordon
would write openly to him on the situation.
The letter was dated 14th December, and in
it Gordon said he expected a crisis within
the next ten days, or about Christmas-day.
He evidently had given up all hope of help
from outside, and asked Watson to say good-

bye to his friends and relations. This agreed with his letter of the 4th November, which said he had provisions enough to hold out until the middle of December, but that after that it would be difficult to do so.

As soon as I had read the letters, I told Boscawen that I intended to carry out the original programme, and go up to Khartum; and I asked him to take over the executive details of the command, as I intended going down the river next morning to see if a force was coming up from Berber, and to go on to Khartum as soon after as I could. I also told Herbert Stewart the same thing.

The position was this. The original programme had failed. It was that Stewart was to occupy Matammeh; then that Beresford was to man the steamers with his Naval Brigade, and take me to Khartum, and that I was to leave Burnaby in command. Burnaby was dead, Stewart danger-

ously wounded, all the officers of the Naval
Brigade killed or wounded except Beresford,
who was ill, and could not walk without assistance. The force had lost more than one-
tenth of its numbers, and was encumbered
by over 100 wounded. It was absolutely
necessary to send a convoy off for provisions
as soon as the camels could travel, and the
horses of the 19th Hussars were too much
done up to reconnoitre any distance from
camp. I had every reason to believe
that forces of the enemy were advancing
against us from the north and south, and
I could not leave the small force in its
position on the Nile without ascertaining
whether it was likely to be attacked. I
knew that Omdurman had fallen, and that
Gordon had expected Khartum to fall
on Christmas-day ; but I also knew that
Khartum was still holding out, and I hoped
that the pressure upon the town would be
relieved by the large number of men sent

H

down by the Mahdi to meet us, and that
news of our victories would have got into
Khartum, and given Gordon and his garrison fresh heart. At any rate there was
nothing to show—and I questioned the com-
manders of the steamers carefully—that the
crisis at Khartum which had been deferred
from the 25th December to the 19th of January would be hurried on, or that a delay of a
couple of days would make much difference.

I also considered that my first duty was
to see that the small force which had been
so roughly handled on its march to the Nile
was safe from immediate attack. The result
of the fight at Abu Klea was known to
Khashm el Mus on the evening of the 17th,
and it was probably known in the Mahdi's
camp and in Khartum on the 19th or
20th; I hoped this would still further delay
the expected crisis. A large body of the
enemy were said to be collected at Sayal,
below Matammeh.

It was these considerations taken together
that made me undertake a reconnaissance
down the river before starting for Khartum. My arrangements were that Barrow's
Hussars were to reconnoitre as far as they
could up the river early in the morning, and
that if they sent back word to say that they
could see nothing of Feki Mustafa's force, I
would start down the river with two steamers
and two companies of the Mounted Infantry.
I sent all Gordon's Journals, &c., back on
board the steamers, as I thought they would
be safer there than on shore in the camp.
When I got down to the new camp on the
river-bank it was quite dark, and I was
pretty tired.

It was now necessary to send an officer
with despatches to Lord Wolseley, and I
selected Pigott of the Mounted Infantry for
this work. But when it came to a question
of mounting him and his escort, we found
that none of the horses could go, they were

so weak, and that even the camels, those
long - suffering animals, required rest and
food ; so his departure had to be put off till
the next night. Before turning in I paid
a short visit to the hospital, and found all
the wounded doing well, in spite of the
shaking they must have had whilst being
carried down to the river ; Crutchley, especially, was very cheery after his amputation.

Jan. 22*d.*—Barrow's scouts having sent
in word to say they could see no trace of an
enemy, we started down the river—three
steamers having got up steam instead of
two. I went in the ʻTalahawiyehʼ with
Beresford, who had to be helped on board,
and was placed on a seat in the cabin, and
two companies of Mounted Infantry under
Major Phipps. The proper commandant
was Nashi Pasha ; but in consequence of
what Gordon had said, I turned him out
and put Khashm el Mus Bey in his place.
Verner went down with Abd ul Hamid Bey

and native soldiers in the 'Bordein,' and the 'Es Safia' followed with her own captain and crew. Before starting I arranged to return at once in case we heard heavy firing, such as would lead us to believe that the camp was being attacked in our absence.

As we steamed down past Matammeh, a few shots were fired at us from the banks, to which our men replied; but I do not think any one was hit. When we were approaching the bank near Sayal, there was some excitement, as the men on the steamers reported that there was a battery in a *sakieh* pit. We found it empty; the gun had probably been taken off to Matammeh. A party was landed and went up to the battery, which they destroyed. It was neatly made in the excavation of an old *sakieh*, and in front of it was a broad sandbank. From this point there was a good view of the district round, and of the clump of palm-trees at Sayal, but we could see no trace of

the enemy said to be assembled at that
place.

We then went on, passing another battery,
this time on the right bank, very cunningly
made, at the water's edge ; and as we were
nearing Shendy, a man waved to us from
the bank. The 'Talahawiyeh' was at once
slowed, and ran in to the bank to take him
on board. He told us that the force from
Berber had halted when it met the fugitives
from Abu Klea ; that there was a large party
in Shendy favourable to the Government ;
and that there were not more than 300 or
400 dervishes in the town.

Meantime Verner had gone on in the
'Bordein,' and seeing us halted, had pulled
up close to the end of the town. He had
then allowed some of the Sudanese to land
and go up to a ruined house near the
town, from which they began to fire at men
in the opposite houses. I was urged to
land our men and try to take Shendy, a

large place twice as big as Matammeh. Of
course I refused, as it would have been
madness to attempt it; and success would
have been practically useless, for Shendy
was on the opposite side of the river to
our camp, and could not have been held.
It was lucky we did not attack, as shortly
after hauling off from the bank, we saw
the Emir Wad Hamza riding in with a lot
of men. He had been up the river watching the steamers, and when they started
down to meet us, he had followed them
and was just arriving. If we had attacked
we should have been caught in a trap.

When we reached the 'Bordein' we
found Verner and his men already retiring,
as the fire had begun to get rather hot.
We went down a little farther, to a large
Government store which was in ruins; and
here we managed to communicate with
another man of Khashm el Mus' tribe, the
Shagiyeh. His evidence was to the same

effect as that of the first man ; it was now therefore certain that we had nothing to fear from any force advancing from the north, at any rate for several days. Before returning, the steamers hauled off into mid-stream and fired from each gun ten rounds of shell, or sixty shell in all, into the town. After this was finished we returned up-stream, making slow progress against the current.

Beresford was, I fear, in much pain, and could not stand up for any length of time, but he was very cheery over it. On the way back he asked me to appoint Mr Ingram, of the 'Duke of Cambridge's Hussars,' to the Naval Brigade, as he had no officers and could not go about himself. To this I was glad to give my consent, and made him an acting - lieutenant Royal Navy on the spot. Ingram had come up the river as the correspondent of some small newspaper, making this an excuse for getting to the front. He had brought out a small steam-launch, but had been obliged to leave the engine in the cataracts, and then by sheer energy got his boat up to Korti. He was a keen soldier, and fought in the front rank as a volunteer in the squares at Abu Klea and Matammeh. At one time he was outside the square at Abu Klea; but always cool and collected, using his rifle with good effect. Many of us had noticed his gallantry, and his quiet determined manner, so that it was a real pleasure to be able to give him some definite position with the force. I hope it may be the means of getting him a commission: men of his stamp are invaluable at critical moments, such as that when the square was broken.

As we neared the lower end of the long island which lay opposite the camp, we saw men crossing in boats to the right bank; and as it was dangerous to allow men, who might creep up and fire into the camp, to

remain on the island, we landed a lot of the
Sudanese to clear the place.   They at once
commenced firing away in the wildest manner; and if they did not hit anybody, they
at least frightened every one off the island.
We got back to camp just at dark.   The
reconnaissance took much longer than I
expected, but we had clearly ascertained
that nothing was to be feared from the
Berber direction.

Whilst we had been away, the garrison
left in camp had at one time expected an
attack, for they had seen large numbers of
the enemy near Matammeh, whom they believed to be reinforcements arriving from
Khartum.   I think they were the same
men we had noticed watching the steamers, with a view to resist a landing if attempted below the town.   Before leaving
the steamer I gave orders for preparations
to be made for a start next day to Khartum.   A good deal had been done towards

putting the camp in a state of defence whilst
we had been away; and the village above,
which was held by the Guards' Camel Regiment, had been made strong enough to
resist any sudden attack.   Unfortunately
Pigott could not get away with the
despatches : the guides were afraid to go
with him, and neither horses nor camels
were in a fit state to make a rapid journey
to Abu Klea.   It was therefore arranged
that he should go out with the convoy
next evening, ride with it to Abu Klea,
and then push on to Korti by himself with
the letters and despatches. Unluckily, as we
afterwards heard, he lost his way, and got
to Jakdul after the convoy; but thence
onward he made a very rapid journey.

The position at Gubat was not a very
good one, but no better could be found near
at hand.   At a distance of half a mile to
a mile from the Nile there is a gravel
terrace, and the intervening space is occu-

pied by a well-cultivated plain watered by
irrigation.   At the end of the plain the
ground falls rapidly to the river, and it was
on this steeper slope that the camp was
pitched.   It was thus quite concealed from
the land side, but exposed to an enemy on
the island opposite.   This latter side was
guarded at first by one of the steamers,
and afterwards by the Egyptians, who were
placed in a small work thrown up on the
island.   I found Stewart had been moved
into the little 'Tewfikiyeh' steamer, where
he is more comfortable.   He seemed more
hopeful about himself.

Jan. 23*d.*—Commenced preparations for
a start at daybreak.   The first point was
to take out the Turco-Egypto-Circassian
"hens," whose removal had been so strongly
insisted upon by Gordon.   This was no light
matter, as the men were mixed up in the
steamers in the most curious way, and it was
difficult to rout them out.   The four steamers

which had come down were the 'Talahawiyeh,' Nashi Pasha; 'Bordein,' Abd ul
Hamid Bey; 'Es Safia,' Mahmud Bey; and
the 'Tewfikiyeh,' Khashm el Mus Bey. After
consultation with Beresford, I determined
to take the two first, as they were the larg-
est boats, and the best protected against the
heavy fire which we now knew we should
have to encounter; but I was much disappointed to find from the captains that in
another twelve days they would not be able
to pass the cataracts. My arrangement was
to place Khashm el Mus in command of the
'Bordein,' and Abd ul Hamid in command
of the 'Talahawiyeh,' and to select crews
and soldiers for them from the Sudanese on
the four ships. We had also to find out the
best pilots for the cataracts, and transfer
them to the two ships. It was very troublesome work, and took Wortley and Gascoigne best part of the day.

By this time I knew that Omdurman

was in the Mahdi's hands, and that we
should have to fight our way into Khartum; and Khashm el Mus told me there
were several batteries on the river similar
to those we had seen yesterday, which we
should have to fight our way past : very
unpleasant works to engage going up-stream.
It was therefore necessary to have the engines overhauled, and as far as possible to
prepare the ships for the heavy fire they
would have to encounter.   The engines
were old and worn, but in fairly good order;
the naval artificers remedied some trifling
defects, and we got a pump from the Royal
Engineers to replace one that had been
broken.   Then we had to get in a supply
of wood for fuel, draw rations, &c., all taking time—so that when the arrangements
were completed it was near sunset, and too
late to start.   We had at first made up our
minds that we should get away by mid-day
or soon after ; but no one who has not at-

tempted it can have any idea of the difficulty of getting natives to work quickly,
especially when orders have to be given
through interpreters. So the hours slipped
by, and we failed to make a start.

The original plan was for Beresford to
man two of the steamers with the Naval
Brigade, mount his Gardner gun on one
of them, and after overhauling them, take
me to Khartum with about fifty men of
the Sussex Regiment. This was now impossible: all the naval officers were killed
or wounded except Beresford, who was himself unable to walk, and many of the best
petty officers and seamen were also gone.
Beresford offered to accompany me; but he
had done himself no good by going down the
river the day before, and there was every
prospect of his getting worse before he was
better. Besides, I felt I could not deprive
the force of its only naval officer, when it
was quite possible the steamers left behind

might have to take part in a fight. Beresford gave me all the assistance and advice
he could whilst lying in hospital, and let me
have two of his artificers. In consequence
of the number of wounded I was unable to
take a surgeon, or even a " dresser," and I
did not feel justified in taking more than
an officer and twenty men as escort.

Lord Wolseley had particularly wished
the escort to enter Khartum in red coats,
and red coats had been especially sent out
for them by the convoy which Burnaby
brought to Jakdul ; but they had disappeared, either lost during the night-march
from Abu Klea, or looted during the night
of the 19th-20th whilst we were away from
the zeribah bivouacking on the bank of the
river. A call was made for red coats, and a
sufficient number were raised from the Guards
and Heavies to clothe all, though some of the
tunics of the Life Guardsmen were rather
too much for the Sussex. By evening all

was ready; the Sussex detachment lay down
just outside the steamers, and I had nothing on shore but my blanket. Orders were
given for steam to be up at daylight. In
the evening the convoy and escort started
for Jakdul to bring up more provisions.
Colonel Talbot went in command, and Pigott of the Mounted Infantry went with
him, carrying despatches.

Jan. 24th.—After all, the steamers were
not ready to start until 8 A.M., but we did
get off then. It was a relief at first to be
quietly seated in a steamer, and to be able
to think over our future proceedings. Now
what was it we were going to do? We
were going to fight our way up the river
and into Khartum in two steamers of the
size of "penny" steamers on the Thames,
which a single well-directed shell would
send to the bottom; with crews and soldiers absolutely without discipline; with
twenty English soldiers; with no surgeon,

I

and with only one interpreter, the faithful
Muhammed Ibrahim, still suffering from a
flesh-wound in the side.

As far as I could make out from the
captains, we should get on very well to
Nasri Island, where the steamers had been
lying; then we should have to pass a battery at Wad Habashi, some very hot places
in the cataracts, a large battery above them,
and after that nothing but musketry until we
got to Halfiyeh, whence we should have to
fight our way into Khartum.   The captains
knew that Omdurman had been taken; and
as the steamers had to pass not far from the
fort when running from the White into the
Blue Nile, they were doubtful about our
being able to run into Khartum, now it was
in the enemy's hands.   They told me, however, that Gordon could see the steamers, or
their smoke, fifteen or twenty miles off, and
I knew that when he saw us he would create
a diversion of some kind.   I hoped to be

able to run in during this diversion; or, if
I could not do that, to land on Tuti Island,
and thence communicate with Gordon.
The appearance of the vessels, and the fact
that the 'Bordein' had been hulled by shot
on her way down, showed the enemy had
some good shots with them.

I was puzzled how to get out of Khartum when I once got in, as the captains
said it would be difficult to get such large
steamers down the cataracts at this time
of year; the only chance would be to run
the gauntlet in one of Gordon's small steamers. The steamers had been prepared by
Stewart,[1] who had, in one of his latest private letters, described himself as Admiral and
Chief Constructor of the Navy. How little
I thought, when reading that letter, that in

[1] This was of course done under General Gordon's directions; but many of the native officers spoke of the close
personal supervision given by Colonel Stewart, who, they
said, was constantly in the dockyard whilst the steamers
were being fitted out.

a few short months he would be gone, and
that I should be going up to Khartum in
one of his steamers ! They were admirably
adapted for the work they had to do,—
rough-and-ready devices, with a thorough-
ness about everything very characteristic of
Stewart.

The two boats were fitted in much the
same way : at the bow a small space was
left for the cable, and then came a rude
turret of baulks of wood fastened together
with iron pins, and built up from the deck
so as to give a gun-platform to fire over
the bulwarks. The turret was not round,
but splay-shaped, to fit the bows ;
it was bullet-proof, but not shot or
Turret.   shell proof, and it was open at top.
In this turret there was one gun firing right
ahead through a port-hole. At the foot of
the turret was the cooking-place, where all
day long the slave-girls were baking dura-
cakes for the soldiers and sailors. How

they never set the ship on fire was always a
mystery to me. Behind this was the hatchway of the fore-hold, and a gangway on
each side for landing; then the foremast,
to which a bird-cage was slung for a look-
out man—a sort of iron bucket; next followed on each side small dirty cabins at
either end of the paddle-boxes; and between the paddle-boxes the midships turret
—a square box, built, like the other, of
baulks of wood pinned together.

The floor of the turret was just high
enough to enable the one gun in it to fire
well over the top of the paddle-boxes; it
had a port on each side, and was reached
from the after-part of the ship by a ladder
which led to a small square hole, through
which it took a moment or two to squeeze
one's self. From the ports one could get out
on to the top of the paddle-boxes. Thus,
any one going to the turret in action was
unpleasantly exposed. Within the turret,

shot, shell, and cartridges were lying about
in a way that would soon have put an end
to a boat not manned by orientals.   After
the turret came the funnel, with many a
bullet-hole through it, and the boiler, partly
above deck, but protected by logs of wood
placed over it.   Then came the hatchway
of the main - hold, and just behind it a
saloon or deck-house, a slight wooden struc-
ture divided into two rooms, and having a
narrow passage running round it.

On the top of the saloon a place had
been prepared for infantry, by making
walls of boiler - plate iron, except at the
entrance.   The wheel was on the top of
this deck - house, and particular care had
been taken to protect the helmsmen as much
as possible.   Behind the deck-house was a
little open space in the stern, with a hatchway leading to a small hold.

Round the sides of the ship the bulwarks
and deck-house were protected by sheets of

boiler-plate iron fixed to wooden stanchions,
except where the cabins and paddle-boxes
came. The plates were just high enough
to allow a man to fire over them, and along
the top of the stanchions ran a wooden
beam sufficiently rais-
ed above the plates to
leave a long loophole.
This gave excellent
cover, and was bullet-proof, except at ranges
under 150 yards. To shot and shell it
offered no protection, and unfortunately it
was broken in several places, especially at
the stern, where some sheets had disappeared; it also left about a foot of the upper
portion of the deck-house quite exposed.

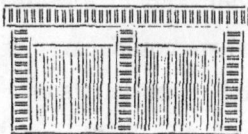

In the fore-hold were the gun and some
of the rifle ammunition, with an enormous
quantity of dura and loot, besides wood for
the steamer. In the main-hold were rifle ammunition, firewood, sacks of dura, bedding,
loot of all kinds, women, a baby or two, and

a herd of goats for milk.   In the after-hold
were the loot and property of the commandant.

In fact every hole and corner below deck
was filled with dura, Indian corn, fuel, and
loot, and on the deck we had as much dura
as we could carry piled up in sacks for the
Khartum garrison.   What with these sacks
and the large number of men on board, it
was no easy matter getting about.   The
filth was something indescribable — the
stench which rose up from the holds over-
powering; and the rats legion and ubiquitous—no place or person was too sacred for
them.

It is difficult to describe the state into
which the Sudanese had brought the steamers during the five months they had lived
as river pirates on the Nile.   The only
part of the boats that had been well
looked after were the engines, which, though
old and wanting a thorough overhauling,

were clean and bright, and worked smoothly. Then the crews and soldiers were a most extraordinary lot. There was first of all the commandant, who was supposed to be in command of the soldiers and of the ship, and who really controlled the movements of the ship, and took command of the soldiers when they landed ; the officer commanding the regulars—all blacks, once slaves ; the officer commanding the Artillery; the officer commanding the Shagiyeh Bashi-Bazuks ; Turkish Bashi-Bazuk officers, who had brought and commanded their own slaves ; the captain who commanded the crew, which was split up into sections under their respective heads ; the chief of the sailors ; the chief of the caulkers, of the carpenters, the woodcutters, &c. ; the *reis* or pilot with his assistants, who navigated the ship ; the helmsmen ; the chief engineer with his assistants, and the stokers and firemen ; and last, not least, the ladies who ground the dura into

meal, and made the great wafer-like dura-
cakes in which the Sudanese delight. The
soldiers were all slaves, and the officers
black, except those of the Artillery, who were
Egyptians. The Bashis were partly Shagiyeh, partly black slaves, and partly half-
caste ; the officers of Bashis were Turks,
Kurds, and Circassians ; the captains and
reises Dongolese ; the sailors blacks, and
the engineers Egyptians.

Such a motley crew, and such a business
getting them to work together, or, in fact,
to work at all ; and as to the noise, it was
sometimes deafening. They were, however,
a cheery, good-humoured lot, much like
spoiled children, and quite amenable to
King Kurbash. Of course, when we got
fairly under way, we found lots of men
who ought not to have come—stowaways
anxious to get up to their families, and
wounded men who had concealed themselves amongst the bags of dura.

To conclude the description, our guns
were what the French call *canons rayés*,
small handy brass pieces, throwing a 9-lb.
shell, and the soldiers were armed with
Remingtons; but instead of a bayonet, each
man had a spear, and many of them swords
as well. Most of the men wore Gordon's
decoration for the siege of Khartum, of
which they were very proud. There was
an abundance of gun and small-arm ammunition, and Gordon had evidently spared no
trouble in making the steamers as good
fighting-boats as possible. If there had
only been officers and men of the Naval
Brigade to man them, it would have been
perfect.

I went in the 'Bordein,' which I was
told was the best and quickest boat, and
had with me Gascoigne and his black servant Suleiman, one sergeant, one lance-
corporal and eight men of the Sussex, one
naval artificer, Muhammed Ibrahim the

interpreter, and my servant Sutton, a driver
R.E. The commander was Khashm el Mus
Bey, the 'Melik' or King of the Shagiyeh
in these parts, a man of about fifty-two
or fifty-three, with greyish beard, rather
short, not very beautiful, but with a certain amount of dignity. He has great influence amongst the Shagiyeh, who have
been settled on the right bank since the days
when Muhammed Ali made a clean sweep
of the people for murdering his son. The
old gentleman was much trusted by Gordon,
to whom he remained loyal under great
temptation. He can neither read nor write;
that is done for him by a sharp little fellow
called Muhammed Bey Abud, grandson of
the commander of the Shagiyeh army which
conquered Dongola the end of last century;
and a certain Sheikh Mahmud, a trusted
messenger of Gordon's, who got shut out
of Khartum when on a mission to Sidi
Osman, the great religious sheikh at Kas-

sala. Of course old Khashm el Mus never does anything except sit on a sofa, whence he gives his orders, whilst smoking, and drinking coffee.

In the saloon were old Khashm, myself, Gascoigne, and Muhammed Ibrahim; in the little room behind, the two servants and the naval artificer; and on the top of the deck-house the ten men of the Sussex, with their arms, ammunition, kits, and food — they were thus in a little citadel, and commanded the whole ship in case of a mutiny or of anything going wrong. No one was allowed to go there except the two helmsmen.

In the 'Talahawiyeh' were Captain Traf-ford, commanding the Sussex detachment, one corporal and nine men, Stuart Wortley with his servant (a Rifleman), one artifi-cer Royal Navy, and a signaller. There was no interpreter, and all orders had to be given by Wortley in forcible Arabic, helped out by strong English and much

vigour of action.   The commander was
Abd ul Hamid Bey, a tall slight man of
prepossessing manner and appearance, who
had brought down a very strong letter
of recommendation from Gordon to Lord
Wolseley, which wound up with words to
the effect that he was the best native he
had met.   He was very young, too young
for the position he was holding, and he had
the petulant manners of a spoiled child,
amusing to watch, but annoying when
work has to be done.   He constantly re-
minded me of Gordon's description of the
" cub," Zebehr's son, in his Sudan letters.
He was fond of dress, and always turning
up in some flowing garment of gorgeous
hue.   He also was a Shagiyeh, and a relation of Khashm's.

The ' Talahawiyeh ' had the same curious
medley of crew and soldiers on board, and
also the Greek who brought down Gordon's
last diary, and who was anxious to rejoin

his family. The Sussex men were posted in
the same position, and all the arrangements
were similar to those on the 'Bordein.' The
'Bordein' had on board 110 black troops
besides the crew; the 'Talahawiyeh' 80
black soldiers on board, but she towed a
large dismasted *nuggar*, or native boat,
filled with dura for Khartum, and carrying between 40 and 50 additional soldiers.

Each of the steamers flew two Egyptian
flags, one at the foremast and one at the
stern. I at first thought of pulling them
down, as I disliked the idea of fighting
under the Egyptian flag; but I had no
others to put in their place, and they were
still the Khedive's steamers. My orders
to the steamers were to make all speed to
Khartum, and to the Sussex not to waste
their ammunition in single shots or on
small groups of men, but directly they got
within range of a battery to fire volleys at
the embrasures : in this way I hoped to

check the enemy's gun-fire, which was the
only thing we really had to fear. The native
troops were quite undisciplined; and as any
attempt to check them was hopeless, I told
them to fire away when any one fired at
them. The 'Talahawiyeh' was to conform
to the movements of the 'Bordein.'

. We steamed steadily on past the end of
the island and the scene of our bivouac on
the night of the 19th, and then got into
fresh ground. About 10.30 a native hailed
us from the right bank, and we stopped to
take him on board. He turned out to be
a friendly. Shagiyeh of Gandattu, who told
us that a short distance ahead there was
a battery with a gun in it. We went on,
keeping close to the bank until we got to a
corner, on rounding which we should see the
battery; then I stopped, and landed Gascoigne with some of the black troops, and
Trafford and Wortley with blacks from the
other boat. It was almost impossible to

keep the blacks in hand, but they went up to the battery and found it empty. The marks of the gun-wheels were quite fresh; and some men who came on board told us that Wad Hamza, the Emir of Shendy, had put the gun there to prevent the steamers from going up, but hearing that they had gone down to Shendy, had taken it out and off to Shendy. Lucky for us, as the battery was well concealed in the bank just above the water-line, and well placed for catching us as we got round the corner. Like all the other batteries it had three embrasures—to give fire up, down, and across the river.

The men who came on board were Shagiyeh, known to Khashm el Mus; and they brought friendly messages from their chiefs, to say that they would join us when the army came up. Our victories had evidently produced a great effect. The enemy estimated their own loss at 3000, and did not seem to realise how severely we had

K

suffered. I gave them all sorts of assur-
ances of good treatment by the army, and
did not forget to send my salams to Sidi
Osman's sisters—those "plucky ladies," as
Gordon calls them. They certainly have
been very plucky, living on in the midst
of the rebellion—avowedly hostile to the
Mahdi, and yet respected by every one.
They owe their safety to their descent from
Muhammed and their close relationship to
Sidi Osman. From this place I sent off a
letter to Gordon to say that we were on
our way.

After we had got our brave "pirates"
on board, we steamed on again, and a little
higher up saw in the distance a large body
of horse and camel-men on the left bank.
These were a portion of Feki Mustafa's force
which, we had heard, was advancing upon
us, and was to have been at Matammeh on
the 21st or 22d. He had halted about
twelve miles from camp—not liking the

stories he had heard of us from men wounded on the 19th in our fight for the Nile.

Feki Mustafa is a Jalin of Zebehr's tribe, married to a Shagiyeh woman related to Khashm el Mus.   He was a man of much repute for sanctity, and had commanded the Arabs on the Omdurman side from the very commencement of the siege of Khartum; but his fighting capacity was not equal to his religious fervour.   He had left Omdurman two days after Nur Angar, whom we fought on the 19th, but had no heart to come on. As this was the third force which the Mahdi had sent against us, we were in great hope that there would be such a sensible diminution of the besieging force as would enable Gordon to make some vigorous sorties to obtain food for his garrison. We were honoured by a few shots, but they fell too short or passed harmlessly overhead; indeed every now and then during

the day stray shots were fired at us from
the left bank, none from the right.

About 12.30 we halted at a deserted
village to take in a store of wood, and
here we had our first experience of the habits
of our Sudani friends. Trafford, Gascoigne,
and Wortley landed with them; but the
blacks were too quick for them, and half
were at once away looting and letting off
their rifles. However, a certain number
were kept to wood-carrying with the sailors:
the wood was obtained by pulling down
the houses. As I was sitting watching
them, a Bashi came and told me they had
found a camel. Did I want it? and should
they bring it on board? I said no; and
off they went. A few minutes after, I went
on shore to hurry them on with the wood,
and the first thing I saw was the camel
— or rather his bones — lying on the
ground; he had been killed, stripped of
his flesh, and fires lighted to roast him.

It was a horrible sight: the blacks wild
with excitement, covered with blood, and
running about with huge pieces of flesh,
which they tore like wild beasts. I was
very angry, and had up some of old
Khashm's myrmidons to administer *kurbash* all round. They grinned as only
niggers can, rushed off to the steamers
with their joints, and then came back to
carry wood. Meantime the three officers
had been up with the men working at the
village, and by "precept and example"
got them to wood-up quicker than, I fancy,
they had ever done before. We then
started again, and kept on till dark, when
we made fast to the right bank near Gos
el Bessabir.

Our progress had been slow, owing to
the heavy loads the steamers were carrying
and to the low state of the water, which
made navigation difficult amongst the sand-
banks. The banks of the river were low,

and on either side there was much cultivated ground—Indian corn and dura—
irrigated by *sakiehs*, and not bearing out
the stories we had heard of the desolation
worked by Khashm el Mus and his " braves."
As soon as the steamers had fastened to the
bank, the blacks landed, lighted their fires,
and began to cook their dinners. Trafford
and Wortley came to dine with us ; and
Abd ul Hamid, Khashm, and Muhammed
Ibrahim fed *à l'Arabe* out of a huge dish
on the floor. Old Khashm has developed
a great weakness for tea sweetened to a
syrupy consistence.

Jan. 25th.—I lay awake for a long time
last night thinking over the situation, and
how Gordon would receive the news, and
what effect it would have on affairs at
Khartum. Buller's calculation was that
Earle would be at Shendy on 5th March,
and Lord Wolseley at Matammeh on the
2d March : more than another month to

wait, and Gordon had given up hope in December. In November we knew that he could only hold out with difficulty after the middle of December, and I had to inform him that we could not relieve him till the middle of March. Then I had to tell him of the rough handling of the little force which had reached the Nile; the losses in officers, and the state of the transport, all of which must delay the relief; and last, my orders to take back the few soldiers I had.

The outlook was not bright; my only hope was that, with the steamers and the few Englishmen, we might make a sortie before I left which would shake the enemy and bring in provisions. I try not to show anxiety. I do not know whether I succeed. Every one else is in high spirits; they think all is finished or nearly so, and that the safety of Gordon and Khartum is assured. I wish I could feel the same,

but I do not see how he is to hold on till
the middle of March.　When I did get to
sleep it was only for a short time, for the
rats held high carnival, races round the
cabin, and my slightly thatched skull was
evidently the landing-place after a jump.
In self-defence I had to muffle myself up,
leaving only a small blow-hole to escape
suffocation.

We made a good start, steam up and off
at daylight, a delightfully fresh morning;
river-banks much the same as yesterday.
In the morning we had to stop for wood,
again taken from a village.　Of course
the Bashis were off after loot or anything
to save themselves the trouble of carrying
wood, but this time we were ready for them.
Ibrahim used his *kurbash* to good purpose,
and Trafford, Gascoigne, and Wortley went
up to the village.　Such a business this
wooding is : first the houses or *sakiehs* have
to be pulled down and carried to the bank,

and then the logs have to be cut up, so as
to go into the furnace, with the roughest of
axes and a couple of cross-cut saws which
have not been " set " for no one knows how
long.

Again *en route*, and passed a strong position at Jebel Tanjur, a small isolated hill
near the bank, close to which the steamers
had to pass. Luckily no one was there to fire
at us. About five miles higher up we came
to the position of Wad Habashi, where the
steamers had had a fight on a previous occasion. At this point the enemy were known
to have two guns, and the steamers were
got ready for action. When we reached the
place we found it deserted—for Feki Mustafa
had taken the guns with him—and passed
without a shot. The position is a strong
one, as the channel runs close to the bank,
and a steamer has to go slowly in consequence of some dangerous rocks. The enemy
had made a small work in the sand with

three embrasures, and a long rifle-trench
on each side : a nasty-looking place, which
we were glad to find unoccupied.

We now had a stretch of three or four
miles of open water in front of us, and on
nearing the head of it the captains wanted
to run in to the bank, as the cataract commenced there, and they said they could not
reach a good place to tie up at before dark.
There was still an hour and a half of daylight, and I pressed them to go on. They
objected; but after much expenditure of
strong language and gesticulation, the captain of the 'Talahawiyeh' said he would go
on, and she started off, the 'Bordein' following. We now entered the long Shabloka
cataract, which consists of open stretches
of water with dangerous rapids in which
there are many rocks. It was exciting
work, and I could not help thinking of
Gordon's "praying up" the nuggars on the
Upper Nile.

All went well until near sunset, when the
'Bordein' struck heavily on a rock at the
head of the last rapid we had to surmount
before getting to a reach of open water.
The 'Talahawiyeh' was 500 or 600 yards
ahead, and got safely to Hassan Island,
where she lay to for the night. We worked
hard under the bright moonlight until past
ten, but could not move the 'Bordein.'
We had anchors out, and hauled, tried
poling, sent out a hawser to a small island
with men to pull upon it—all to no purpose. We did our best to help, and the
blacks worked fairly well; but it was difficult
to convey orders and get work done with
only one interpreter—all we could do was
to give instructions and let them work in
their own way. About 9 P.M. Gibril, the
captain of the 'Talahawiyeh,' came down
with men to help. He was said to be the
most experienced of the captains, but even
he could do nothing. The men had been

working for six hours to no purpose, so we
laid out anchors, and waited for morning.
It was a novel sensation going to sleep in
a steamer hanging on a sunken rock, with
water running like a mill - race all round
her. If she slips during the night, will
the hawser stand the jerk? That was the
question.

All through the day occasional shots were
fired at us from the left bank. Every man
working a *sakieh* seemed to have a rifle and
to take a pot-shot at the steamers. Of course
the blacks replied with a fusilade, but I do
not think they hurt any one, and no one was
touched on the steamers. It kept up the excitement, and showed that the tribes to the
west were hostile. I was a good deal in the
fore part of the ship whilst the men were
trying to get her off, and was much amused
at the *nonchalant* way in which the slave-
girls went on cooking their dura - cakes.
They are at it all day long—no rest. First

the dura is ground between two stones—not
circular ones as in Palestine, but straight
pieces of stone—one rubbed against the
other; then the meal is mixed with water
to the consistency of thick porridge; and
lastly a great lump of it is thrown on a
large circular iron dish heated by a wood-
fire. With a little stick the girl dexterously
manipulates the dough so that it covers the
whole plate like a thin wafer; there is a
noise of frizzling and frying, and in a moment the finished cake is torn off ready for
eating. They are not as good as wheaten
cakes, but we found them a pleasant change
from the hard ration-biscuit.

Jan. 26*th.*—Rats had another race-meet-
ing last night. We were all astir at the
first streak of dawn, to make a last effort
to get the ship off, little thinking of the
awful tragedy which was then being enacted
at Khartum. After talking the matter
over with the captains, we determined to

shift all the stores and ammunition aft, then to land the soldiers on a small sand-bank, and pass a hawser to them to haul upon from the starboard quarter; and finally, to put out an anchor on the starboard quarter also, upon which the Sussex men and those left in the ship might pull. This took a long time; the live shell, the gun cartridges and ammunition had to be carefully handled, and when they were moved the soldiers had to be landed in two small boats over a nasty rapid piece of water. It was near nine before all was ready and the signal was given to pull, but she did not respond. Then we tried "Turn astern full speed and pull together." I was watching a mark on the shore; there was a moment of suspense, then I saw a slight move, followed by a shout of "Stop her," and then "Turn ahead full speed"—all the orders are in English—and we were free again, quivering in the rapid.

water.   Great excitement, the niggers caper-
ing about like Robinson Crusoe's man Friday,
and earnest thankfulness on our part.

It was no easy matter getting the men
on board again and picking up our anchor,
but at last we steamed slowly on and were
soon beside the 'Talahawiyeh.' Here we had
a consultation, for the most difficult part of
the cataract was in front of us.   The result
was that the two captains were to take the
'Bordein' first through the Shabloka passage,
and then return to bring
up the other boat.   We
started from *A*, and followed the eastern branch
through some nasty bro-
ken water with many
pointed rocks peeping
out of it.   We got on very well until we
reached the point *B* and could see open
water beyond, when bump went the old
steamer on a sandbank with a crash which

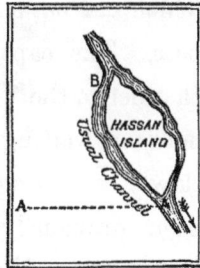

set everything on the dance, and we were
hard and fast again.

We made the soldiers jump out into the
shallow water, and try to heave her off, and
used our poles as well, but still she stuck.
Then the captain went out in the small
boat to sound the passage, and we could
see by his sounding-pole that there was no
chance of our getting through. It was too
clear that the capricious river had thrown
up a sandbank across the usual channel,
which our heavily laden steamers could not
pass. The captain went down the western
channel to the 'Talahawiyeh,' and after long
hours of waiting and watching, we saw her
slowly steaming up, her soldiers having
been previously landed on the island to
march up. She came to an anchor the
other side of the sandbank, and the captains
then came on to us in a small boat.

After some trouble we got the 'Bordein'
off the bank. We then landed the black

soldiers to lighten the ship, and ran down
through the cataract to the mouth of the
other channel. After about fifty yards we
got to a very awkward place—swift water
between two rocks, and only just room
for the steamer to pass; then we had
some ugly turns between rocks in rapid
water. Altogether it was very exciting, and
one could not help admiring the way in
which the captains and *reises* worked the
boat. It was slow work, and we only
reached the 'Talahawiyeh' a little before
sunset, too late to get the soldiers on board
and pass the gorge through the mountains,
which we now saw close in front of us.

It was a most unlucky day. We had
worked hard, and yet at nightfall we were
only three miles above the place where the
'Talahawiyeh' had passed the previous night.
We all abused the Nile pretty freely when
we met for dinner in the evening. We had
expected opposition in this part of the cat-

L

aract, but luckily no shots were fired, except
a few harmless ones in the morning.   Cannot make this out, as there is such splendid
cover on the banks for an enemy; they
might fire all day and not be touched by
the men on the steamers.

The island we were anchored off was
called Hassan Island, one of the ninety-nine
islands and islets of the same name said to
stud the cataract north of Shabloka.   They
are prettily wooded: sometimes the vegetation is very thick and dense; and what
with bright sun, green vegetation, rushing
water, rocks, and yellow sand, there is more
picturesqueness than we have seen elsewhere
on the Nile.   During the course of the evening two Shagiyeh came on board, friends
and relations—they appear to be all related
here—of Khashm el Mus.   They reported
that for the last fifteen days there had been
hard fighting round Khartum — Gordon
always victorious; that the advance of the

English was much dreaded; and that the
Shagiyeh were only waiting for the turn
of the tide to join the English. We have
a shrewd suspicion they will swim with
the tide whichever way it turns. Evidently, as we thought, the Mahdi was
fighting hard to get into Khartum before
we got there, and Gordon gallantly holding
his own. We little dreamt all was then
over.

Jan. 27th.—Started at daylight. We
soon passed Shabloka—a narrow passage
between rocks, which gives its name to the
cataract—and almost immediately entered
a mountain-gorge, where the river is not
more than 300 yards wide, and runs swiftly
for three or four miles between steeply ris-
ing and in some places abrupt hills. Now
we shall get " slated," I thought, if there is
any one there : a few good shots might
have picked off every one on deck. I told
them to drive the engines as hard as they

could, and the Sussex men to reply to any
shots by volleys. Again there was no one.
We were astonished at our good luck, and
began to have a little contempt for an
enemy who neglected to occupy such
splendid positions.

Above the gorge, which was not unlike
some parts of the Danubian " Iron Gates,"
and nearly opposite Jebel Royan, we stopped
on the left bank to take in wood at a place
called Gos Nefîsa. Jebel Royan is an isolated hill, from the top of which we were
told Khartum could be seen. As we were
now well within the enemy's country, we
had to take more precaution, and occupy
the heights round the deserted village
where the men were pulling down the
houses for firewood. No one was in sight
at first; but before we had finished there
were a few dropping shots, which did no
harm. The people apparently had only
just left; and a lot of the blacks, includ-

ing officers, began coming down to the
steamers laden with loot of the most mis-
cellaneous kind, from goats to native bed-
steads. This was too much; so I went on
shore with old Khashm, and as every one
came up with his load of loot he was made
to throw it away and bend his back to the
kurbash,—officers and men, we made no
exception,—and a good many of them got
a second dose from the ever-active Ibrahim.
The village was some distance off, and it
was hot work; but at last all the wood we
could lay hold of was got on board, and we
steamed away.

After passing Jebel Royan the banks
again became flat, with the same kind of
cultivation, and we then got into another
bit of cataract; but by 2 P.M. we were
clear of it, and steaming up open water
against a moderate current. During the
morning, after passing the gorge, there
had been a little desultory firing; but it

now became more frequent, and continued until half an hour before sunset. The blacks replied with a will, ever ready for a chance of letting off their rifles. One shot came in through the deck-house close to my cheek, but it was nearly spent, and the little splinters of wood which struck me did not cut. We kept on until dark, and then moored to the left bank, in front of a deserted village, about one-third of a mile from the river, and opposite Tamaniat. We at once commenced taking in all the wood we could stow away on the steamers,[1] and the men were kept working at this until 1 A.M. They were very lazy, and a good deal of driving had to be done. Gascoigne, Trafford, and Wortley were out pretty nearly the whole time; and the first was, as usual,

---

[1] The quantity of wood burned by the river steamers was out of all proportion to the work got out of them. It used to be said of the 'Nassif Kheir,' employed on the river between Dongola and Korti, that she burned as much fuel as a line-of-battle ship.

indefatigable in his efforts to get work out of the blacks. Some of the Sussex men were also out on picket, and we took every precaution to avoid surprise.

During the afternoon a man on the left bank shouted out to us that a camel-man had just passed down with the news that Khartum was taken and Gordon killed. We did not believe it, nor did Khashm el Mus, who said that such reports had been flying about for the last two months. We dined together in high spirits at the prospects of running the blockade next day, and at last meeting General Gordon after his famous siege. We were curious to see the way in which he kept his people together under the stress of actual siege, for we had not found it easy to control our modest force on the two steamers.

Jan. 28*th.*—Started at 6 A.M. My orders were, the 'Bordein' to lead, the 'Talahawiyeh' to conform to her movements; the

Sussex men to fire volleys at the embrasures of the batteries, which were also to be engaged by the guns of the steamers; the blacks to fire away as hard as they could; the 'Bordein' to go ahead full speed into Khartum, followed by her consort. Wortley and his signaller, who had a heliostat, were to try and attract Gordon's attention. At 7.30 we passed Jebel Seg et Taib, a steep hill close to the bank of the river, where there had been at one time a battery with guns, to prevent the passage of the steamers up and down the river. It was a good position, and, luckily for us, unoccupied. We went on past Abu Alim, where one of the Mahdi's chief emirs lives, and soon after could see Khartum in the far distance above the trees of Tuti Island. About this time a Shagiyeh on the right bank shouted out to the 'Talahawiyeh' to stop, and told them that Khartum had been taken and Gordon killed two days before.

Occasional firing had been going on all the morning, but as we approached Fighiaiha the enemy opened a regular fusilade. The fight had now commenced, and I went with Khashm and Ibrahim to the midship turret, where I remained throughout the action. Gascoigne joined us shortly afterwards, and was there or with the Sussex on the deck-house. In the turret I was close to the captain and *reis*, and also to the engineer, so that I could give orders at once. It made a capital conning tower, for by standing on a stool and looking over, one could see all round. The tower was also bullet-proof, an advantage which old Khashm seemed to appreciate, for he doubled himself up in a corner, and only moved to get out of the way of the gun.

When we came full in sight of Halfiyeh I noticed that the palm - grove had been burned and the houses wrecked—a picture of the desolation of war — and also that

there were several large boats lying by the
bank.   I called Khashm's attention to this,
and he at once replied, "Gordon's troops
must be there, as the Mahdi has no boats."
Directly after, a heavy fire was opened upon
us from four guns and many rifles at from
600 to 700 yards.   The guns were well placed,
one in a *sakieh* pit, two in a little battery
above, and one in the village.   The bullets began to fly pretty thickly, tapping like
hail against the ship's sides, whilst the
shells went screeching overhead or threw up
jets of water in the stream round us.   Our
men replied cheerily, and the gun in the
turret was capitally served by the black
gunners under their captain Abdullah Effendi, who laid the gun each time and fired it
himself.   The gunners, who had nothing on
but a cloth round their waists, looked more
like demons than men in the thick smoke ;
and one huge giant was the very incarnation
of savagery drunk with war.   The shooting

was fairly good, and we heard afterwards
that we had dismounted one of the guns in
the battery; but at the time we could not
see the effect. After we had run the gauntlet and the fire was turned on our consort,
the Sudanese sent up a wild cry of delight,
raising their rifles in their hands and shaking them in the air. It was a strange weird
sight, these black savages with their blood
up, quivering with excitement.

I now had leisure to watch the 'Talahawiyeh' coming through the thick of it, scath-
less as we had done, the red flag streaming
bravely above the smoke, which hung in a
dense cloud round her. The firing now
ceased for a few minutes, and we could see
the large Government House at Khartum
plainly above the trees. Khashm was very
anxious to know whether we could see the
Egyptian flag, which he said Gordon always
kept flying; but neither Gascoigne nor I
could see a trace of one anywhere. Khashm

now began to get anxious, and said he felt
certain something must have happened at
Khartum, and that the place must be in
the Mahdi's hands, otherwise there would
have been no boats at Halfiyeh, and the flag
would be flying. I could not believe this;
at any rate, we could not stop now until we
were certain all was over.

We had only a short respite, for, directly
after passing Shamba, two guns on the right
bank opened upon us, with a heavy rifle-
fire from both banks, and this was kept up
until we came within range of the guns
at Omdurman. When about half-way up
Tuti I thought for a moment that the island
was still in Gordon's hands. A sort of dike
ran along the edge of the island, and behind
this there was a long line of men firing away
as hard as they could. I heard the bullets
singing overhead, and saw them strike the
sand amongst the enemy's sharpshooters on
the opposite bank, and thought they were

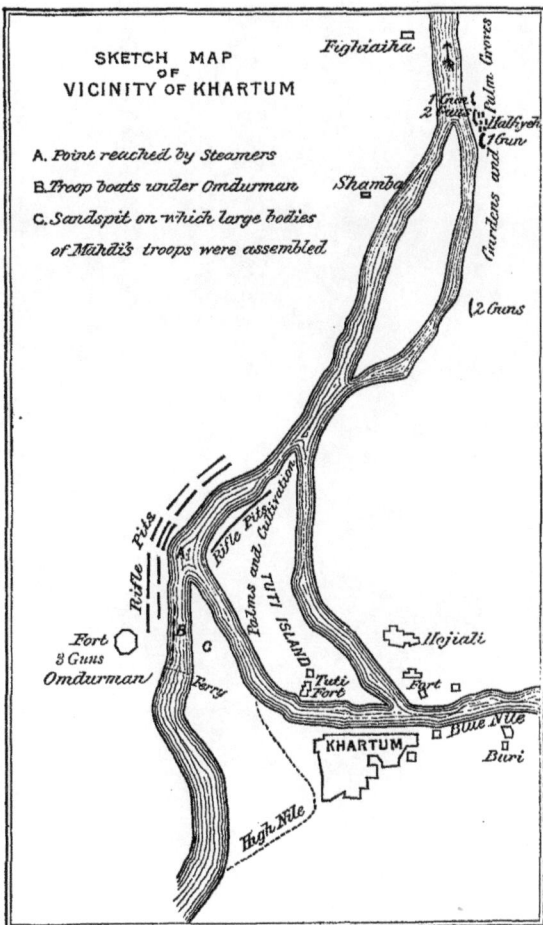

SKETCH MAP
OF
VICINITY OF KHARTUM

A. *Point reached by Steamers*
B. *Troop boats under Omdurman*
C. *Sandspit on which large bodies
of Mahdi's troops were assembled*

Fighaika

1 Gun
2 Guns

Halfiyeh
1 Gun

Gardens and Palm Groves

Shamba

2 Guns

Rifle Pits

Rifle Pits

Rifle Pits and Cultivation

Palms and Cultivation

TUTI ISLAND

Mojiali

Fort
3 Guns
Omdurman

Ferry

*Tuti
Fort*

Fort

Blue Nile

Buri

KHARTUM

High Nile

To face p. 172.

helping us. I then ordered the steamer to run in close to the bank, stop, cease firing, and ask for news. This we did, getting within 60 or 70 yards. I felt so persuaded at first that they were Gordon's men that I got outside the turret, but the only reply to our shouts was a sharper and better directed fire, which soon drove me inside again.

It was clear that the enemy's riflemen were on Tuti; but Khartum might still be holding out—so after a delay of about a quarter of an hour we went on, old Khashm protesting it was all up, and predicting terrible disaster to ourselves. No sooner did we start upwards than we got into such a fire as I hope never to pass through again in a "penny steamer." Two or more guns opened upon us from Omdurman fort, and three or four from Khartum or the upper end of Tuti; the roll of musketry from each side was continuous; and high above that could be heard the grunting of a Norden-

feldt or a mitrailleuse, and the loud rushing
noise of the Krupp shells, fired either from
Khartum itself or from the upper end of
Tuti Island.

We kept on to the junction of the two
Niles, when it became plain to every one that
Khartum had fallen into the Mahdi's hands;
for not only were there hundreds of dervishes ranged under their banners, standing
on the sandspit close to the town ready to
resist our landing, but no flag was flying
in Khartum and not a shot was fired in
our assistance; here, too, if not before, we
should have met the two steamers I knew
Gordon still had at Khartum.   I at once
gave the order to turn and run full speed
down the river.   It was hopeless to attempt
a landing or to communicate with the shore
under such a fire.

The sight at this moment was very
grand : the masses of the enemy with their
fluttering banners near Khartum ; the long

rows of riflemen in the shelter-trenches at
Omdurman; the numerous groups of men
on Tuti; the bursting shells, and the water
torn up by hundreds of bullets and occasional heavier shot,—made an impression
never to be forgotten. Looking out over
the stormy scene, it seemed almost impossible that we should escape.

Directly we turned round, the Sudanese,
who had been wild with excitement, and
firing away cheerily, completely collapsed.
Poor fellows! they had lost wives, families,
and all they possessed. Khashm el Mus
sank into a corner of the turret with his
mantle wrapped round his head, and even
the brave gunner-captain forsook his gun.
"What is the use of firing?" he said; "I
have lost all." For a few moments we could
get nothing out of him; but by dint of per-
suasion, and I am afraid some swearing—is
it not Kinglake who notices the forcible
character of Englishmen's language in action?

—we got him at last to fire; and then, the devil once roused, he served his gun steadily until we had run the gauntlet again and were out of range of the guns of Halfiyeh.

As we passed the 'Talahawiyeh,' which had been aground off Tuti for a few minutes, we shouted to her to turn and follow; and just at this moment we saw a man on a white camel come down to the edge of the river below Omdurman with a flag of truce. He waved and beckoned to us, but as the firing kept on as briskly as ever, we took no notice of him. Whilst we were off Omdurman the small boat we were towing was sunk by a shell, and a fragment of a shell went through the funnel, cutting the stay and letting a rush of flame out, which soon set fire to the large wooden block left swinging in the air. I was rather anxious, as the sparks began to fly about, and the deck was littered with open ammunition-boxes; but on calling for help, a plucky Sudan soldier jumped up, and after a few minutes managed to get down the flaming bit of wood and throw it overboard. If an Englishman, he would have had the Victoria Cross. He was afterwards shot, just as we were getting out of danger.

We all had narrow escapes. I was struck just above the knee by a spent shot which had got through a weak point in the turret; and my field-glass, an old friend of twenty-five years, sent out to me in America, was broken in my hand as I was resting it on the top of the turret. Gascoigne was as imperturbable as ever; he is about the coolest man under fire I have ever seen. Muhammed Ibrahim, the interpreter, was invaluable, always keeping the Sudanese up to the mark, and fully exposing himself—a good proof that every Egyptian is not a coward; and best of all, he did not lose heart when we turned to run down.

The 'Talahawiyeh' was struck by a solid

M

shot, and a shell bursting just in front of the deck-house, sent in a shower of fragments which played much havoc with the fittings, but hurt no one. Another shell burst overhead, and the burning fuse which fell on board was at once picked up and thrown overboard by the drummer of the Sussex. The Sussex men were very steady, and must have done much execution amongst the crowded ranks of the enemy; Trafford told me he saw many of them fall.

When we got clear of the last guns it was past four o'clock, so that for four hours we had been continuously engaged with the enemy's batteries: lucky for us their gunners were such bad shots. I could not help feeling much for poor old Khashm, who, when he got to the cabin, entirely collapsed, rolled himself in a rug, and then coiled himself in a corner, oblivious to all that was going on. The others were af-

fected in much the same way; quite upset, and good for nothing. They knew too
well the fate of their wives and families,
the spoil of the conquerors, sold into
slavery or mated to some wild Arab from
Kordofan.

To me the blow was crushing. "Khartum fallen and Gordon dead"—for I never
for a moment believed he would allow himself to fall into the Mahdi's hands alive—
such was the ending of all our labours and
of his perilous enterprise. I could not
realise it, and yet there was a heavy feeling
at the heart telling of some awful disaster.
For months I had been looking forward to
the time when I should meet Gordon again,
and tell him what every one thought of his
splendid defence of Khartum—and now all
was over; it seemed too cruel to be true.
I think I should have collapsed like Khashm
el Mus if I had not had to think of getting
the steamers down the cataracts, which I

knew, from what the captains said coming up, would be a difficult if not dangerous business.

At dark we made fast to an island about twelve miles south of Jebel Royan, and I sent out two messengers dressed in the Mahdi's uniform,—one to go to Khartum to ascertain the fate of Gordon, the other to collect information. The latter on his return said he had met a Jali, who told him that on the night of the 26th (*i.e.*, the night of our 25th-26th) Khartum had fallen through the treachery of Faraj Pasha, who commanded the regular troops, and Ahmad Bey Jalabi, the mudir of the town, and that Gordon was dead. He also said that on the 27th the Mahdi entered Khartum, prayed in the principal mosque, and returned to Omdurman, giving the town up to three days' pillage.

This confirmation of the news quite finished the natives; the dull, heavy weight

of despair seemed to settle down upon
them, and they looked as men who have
no longer an interest in life. Neither
Khashm nor any of the native officers
would touch food, and our own meal was
not a lively one; we felt the reaction
from the excitement of the fight, when
hope was strong, to the bitter sense of
failure, though it was from no fault of our
own. Perhaps I felt it more keenly than
the others, as I was able more fully to
realise what the death of Gordon and the
fall of Khartum meant, and I had lost a
personal friend for whose character I had
always felt the warmest admiration. The
great point now, however, was to get down
to Gubat as quickly as possible. The condition of the men gave great cause for
anxiety, but I hoped that a night's rest
would give them more heart. As a pre-
cautionary measure, we had a Sussex sentry on the paddle-box, with orders to

shoot any one who attempted to leave
the ship.

The reasons which led me to the conclusion that Khartum had fallen were, that no
Egyptian flag was flying from any place in
or near Khartum, though we all searched
carefully, and were quite near enough to have
distinguished a flag with the naked eye; the
large number of the enemy on the Khartum
side of the Blue Nile close to the town; the
heavy fire brought to bear upon us from
Tuti Island, a place the occupation of which
by the enemy implied the fall of Khartum;
the absence of any counter-attack on the
part of the town, such as I knew Gordon
would have made had he held the place, and
the non-appearance of his steamers in the
reach of the Blue Nile in front of Khartum
where we expected to find them; the large
boats we had seen at Halfiyeh; and the
presence under the guns of Omdurman of a
number of the troop-boats or barges speci-

ally constructed by Gordon for the protection of his troops when he sent them up the river to forage or fight. They were curious affairs,—a sort of boathouses, protected with boiler-plate iron. They looked something like Chinese boathouses as seen in pictures, and it struck me at the time that the idea was perhaps taken from them. None of us had the least doubt about the fall of Khartum. There was some speculation as to Gordon's fate; but I never had any hope myself.

Jan. 29*th.*—We had much to do last evening. First, the wounded had to be attended to—Gascoigne and Wortley doing their best to supply the place of surgeons. Luckily there were no very severe cases, and a nigger is really like a bit of india-rubber; it is perfectly extraordinary to see the way in which they bear their wounds, and the rapidity with which they heal up. The captain of the 'Talahawiyeh' was shot

in the arm ; another through the chin,—and
so on. They all seemed thankful to have
their wounds dressed, and were quite cheery
and uncomplaining. Then we had a long
conference with the captains and *reises*, who
raised great difficulties about passing the
cataracts at this time of year in our large
heavily weighted steamers. It must be
said for them that the Nile was lower than
usual this year; that, as we found on our
return to Gubat, there was a fall of three
feet in a single night whilst we were up the
river; that it was not the custom to send
the larger steamers such as we were on
down the cataracts at this season ; and that
the boats, laden as they were with dura
and the iron plates of the armour, besides
guns and ammunition, were drawing much
more water than usual. I promised each
of the captains £100, and each of the *reises*
£50, if they managed to get the boats down
safely ; and also told them that they might

throw as much of the dura we had brought up for the Khartum garrison overboard as they liked.

We did not get off this morning until 7 A.M., as the float of one of the paddles had got loose, and the iron rod that held it was bent and took some time to straighten. We also had to stop up a lot of holes where bullets had gone through the hull close to the water-line ; they seemed to be bullets from the Nordenfeldt. The way the sides of the boat had been peppered was something to see. At 8.30 the ' Bordein' struck a sandbank ; but we got her off in half an hour. At 11 the steamers stopped for the *reises* and captains of the two steamers to hold a consultation about the cataract, and we then threw overboard a large quantity of the dura, much to the grief of the owners.

At 12.30 we stopped again at the head of the first dangerous piece of cataract, the captains and *reises* declaring that each

steamer must be taken down singly by all
the captains and *reises*.   They were clearly
much alarmed, completely upset by the
events of yesterday, and quite off their
heads.   We could do nothing but drive
them to go on.   The 'Talahawiyeh' was
just shoving off, when Abd ul Hamid Bey
jumped overboard and came walking up the
bank to us in a state of excitement.   It
appears that Wortley had been trying to
rouse him to a sense of the necessity of
doing something.   This the spoiled child
resented, and in a fit of petulance jumped
overboard.   I pitched into him ; but he was
hopeless, and soon rolled himself up by old
Khashm, who has not eaten, and hardly
looked up, since he collapsed yesterday.

The 'Talahawiyeh' was taken down the
rapid in safety, and then the captains
and *reises* came for the 'Bordein.'   We
were soon beside our consort, and sent her
own captain and *reis* on board her, whilst

Abd ul Hamid remained with us. We were
now in open water, going along well, and
I had great hope of getting through the
gorge before dark; but about 4.30 the 'Talahawiyeh,' then leading, struck heavily on a
sunken rock, and immediately began to sink.
We did not notice anything was very wrong
until we passed her, when Wortley shouted
out the dismal news. I at once brought the
'Bordein' up at a little island below, and
Gascoigne went in our small boat to assist. The accident occurred just opposite
Jebel Royan. It appears that the rock lay
in mid-stream in front of a sandbank, and
the accident was caused by a dispute between the captain and *reis* as to which side
of the sandbank they should take the
steamer. The captain held up his hand one
way, the *reis* the other, and the helmsman,
puzzled what to do, kept on straight and
hit the rock. I asked Trafford and Wortley
whether they thought there had been any foul

play; and they both said that, as far as they
could judge, it was pure accident. After-
events, however, gave it a different appearance. The water rushed in quickly, and
the steamer settled down between two rocks.
There was no panic; but the Sudanese and
crew seemed stupefied by late events, and
the native officers were so upset that they
appeared to care little what happened to
them or to the ship.

By great exertion Trafford and Wortley
managed to get the men, the two guns,
the men's arms, kits, rations, and some
boxes of small-arm ammunition, into the
large nuggar they were towing, and before
sunset they had dropped down to us. The
natives bivouacked on the island, whilst
Trafford, Wortley, and the Sussex men joined
us on the 'Bordein.' All the gun ammunition and much of the small-arm ammunition was lost; but we were fortunate not to
lose any lives and to save as much as we

did. Trafford and Wortley acted with great promptitude when the steamer struck, and it is entirely due to their exertions that so much was saved. A few shots were fired at us during the day from both banks, but no one was hit.

In the evening I was told that a messenger from the Mahdi wished to come on board with a letter. As I wanted to find out what had happened at Khartum, I determined to receive him. He turned out to be the same man who had come down to the river at Omdurman, and he had followed us all the way on his white camel. He was, like the Mahdi, a Dongolawi, a certain Feki Abd er Rahman, dressed in the Mahdi's uniform. We were much struck by his quiet manner, the business-like way in which he performed his mission, and his belief in the righteousness of the Mahdi's cause.

The letter [1] was addressed to the British

[1] Appendix VIII.

and Shagiyeh officers : it summoned us to
surrender; told us that Khartum was taken
and Gordon killed ; promised a safe-conduct
to any one who wished to verify the fact ;
invited the English to become Moslems if
they wished for peace, and promised protection to Khashm el Mus and his men if they
submitted. I declined to give an answer
to the letter, but Khashm el Mus seemed
to think one was necessary. He urged
very strongly that we should be entirely
at the mercy of the enemy whilst passing
through the gorge and the cataract, and
proposed to throw them off by a ruse, and
to answer that he would not give himself
up unless the Mahdi sent him a special
safe-conduct and promise of safety. If this
were sent he would give us and the steamer
up to Feki Mustafa at Wad Habashi, where,
we now heard, guns had been mounted and
a force assembled to stop our progress.

I could not help seeing that the slightest

opposition in the cataracts would be fatal
to us, and felt deeply the responsibility I
was under for the safety of all those on
board ; but for a long time I could not
consent to such an answer being sent.   At
last, however, feeling sure of Khashm, who
was too deeply compromised with the Mahdi
to give himself up, and believing that by
holding pistols to the captains' heads we
could force them to run full speed past the
battery, as Khashm el Mus promised to do,
I allowed him to send any answer he wished,
on condition that we English were not
implicated in the ruse.

The letter was seen by Ibrahim, who
told me that Khashm said he would give
himself and us up to Feki Mustafa at Wad
Habashi, if the Mahdi sent him a special
safe-conduct under his seal.   The messenger
said that Gordon was alive at Omdurman,
wearing the Mahdi's uniform.   This I
knew must be untrue, as I was quite cer-

tain Gordon would never submit to that indignity. He also told us that Khartum had been taken without fighting, but that the garrison on Tuti having refused to submit, had been put to the sword. We had some talk with the messenger, who had the Mahdi's programme by heart. They were going to Cairo, then to Stambul, Rome, and eventually to overrun all countries. Wortley remarked that that would take a long time ; to which he neatly replied, time was no object — they could wait any number of years. He also exhorted us to become Moslems, and no longer attempt to resist the irresistible power of the Mahdi.

Suggestions were made to seize the Mahdi's messenger, but he had performed his mission in such a fearless way, and shown such complete trust in us, that I would not allow it.

Two or three Shagiyeh came on board, and had long talks with Khashm el Mus

and Abd ul Hamid. They said they were
going to throw in their lot with the
Mahdi, and advised Khashm to do the
same. Ibrahim was now invaluable, going
about amongst the men, and never allowing
any secret conversations. I sent out two
men to gain information, and late at night
one of them came back and had a long talk
with Khashm el Mus over the situation.
It was the same story : Khartum taken and
Gordon killed; many of the Shagiyeh with
their families killed in Khartum ; promises
held out to Khashm that his family would
be spared if he surrendered. He evidently
believed they had already been killed. I
placed sentries over the captains and *reises,*
with orders to shoot them if they attempted
to escape; but as they are all as much at
home in the water as fish, it is difficult to
prevent desertion. One man managed to
get away from the shipwrecked crew on the
island—our first desertion. I only wonder

N

more did not go; but these blacks are
curious fellows — one can never say what
they will or will not do.

Jan. 30*th.* — Daybreak was very welcome when it came, and we at once commenced preparations for descending another
bad piece of cataract. Large sweeps were
rigged out on the nuggar, and she was
sent on ahead, and we followed in safety.
At the foot of the cataract we picked up
the nuggar, and then went through the
gorge, where, to our great surprise, we
found no one to oppose us. We had now
arrived at the place where we had passed
the night of the 26th-27th, at the top of
the most dangerous portion of the cataract,
and stopped to land all the men and get
rid of as much of the remaining dura and
loot as we could.

The nuggar was again sent on, and told
to wait for us at the end of the island,
where the ' Talahawiyeh ' had made fast on

the night of the 25th. There was a very
strong wind blowing at the time, and it
unfortunately drove us so firmly aground
that we were over an hour getting off. The
men worked famously; the black sailors
and soldiers, who had regained their spirits,
jumped into the water and began heaving
her off with their backs. Some of the
Sussex men shoved with the poles, whilst
others pulled on a hawser made fast to
an anchor. I began almost to despair of
getting her off; when a vigorous pull, as a
momentary lull came in the wind, moved
her, and we were clear. Then came the
narrow rocky cataract, as to the safe passage
of which I was very anxious and a little
dubious.

The captains and *reises* worked admirably,
and we got safely through by going down
stern first, and using hawsers, sometimes
from one and sometimes from both quarters,
made fast to anchors or rocks in the stream,

so as to steady her in her descent. In places our engines had to keep turning ahead, so as to let the steamer go down by inches. I was on the paddle-boxes with the captains, watching them closely, and had some anxious moments; but at last we got safely through. This had taken a long time, so that after we had got our men on board again and picked up the nuggar, we were only able to go a short distance farther, and anchored for the night a little above the place where we had run aground on the 25th. We stopped in mid-stream, to be safe against any attack.

We were thankful to have got down thus far in safety, as half-a-dozen good shots would have stopped us whilst we were lowering the ship down the cataract. We attributed the absence of opposition to Khashm el Mus's ruse and the enemy's belief that they would catch us at Wad Habashi. We were much pleased with the

evident care and skill which the captains
and *reises* had shown in the bad parts of
the cataract.   I called them into the cabin,
complimented them on their skill, and
renewed my promise of a large present on
our safe arrival at Gubat.   I felt, too, much
more confidence in their loyalty; for I
thought that if they had intended to play
us false they would have carried out any
design they had before bringing us down
through the cataract.

I had noticed during the day that Abd ul
Hamid's demeanour towards us had quite
changed.   He was no longer friendly, but
kept to himself, and rarely came into the
cabin.   I thought it was sulkiness — the
petulance of a spoiled child—partly due to
the loss of his ship, and partly to what had
occurred yesterday.   I told Ibrahim to keep
an eye on him during the day.   Just before we anchored, however, Suleiman, Gascoigne's black servant, told us that Abd ul

Hamid wanted to wreck the 'Bordein,' but
that Khashm el Mus had stopped the con-
spiracy. We tried to get out of Suleiman
where and how he had heard this. But,
either through fear or stupidity, he would
not say; and I must confess that I hardly
credited the story, after the very strong
terms in which Gordon had written about
him. After-events, I fear, showed Suleiman
must have been right. After that I kept a
good watch on Abd ul Hamid.

In the evening two Shagiyeh came on
board with a story that Gordon was alive
and shut up in the stone Catholic church
with some Greeks and faithful Shagiyeh. I
did not believe the story; but there was
sufficient foundation for it, in the known
fact that Gordon would try to do this, as
he had placed all his ammunition in the
church, and prepared it for defence. Against
the story was, that we were near enough to
the church on the 26th to have seen any

firing from it had it been held, and that the building could not long have withstood the guns the Mahdi could have brought against it after he had taken Khartum. Another piece of news they told us was, that the English had taken Matammeh, after three days' fighting and in spite of the reinforcements which had been sent to the garrison from Berber; also, that the English were swarming across the desert like ants.

This news, though untrue, was very seasonable; and I have no doubt it partly saved us, by confirming Khashm el Mus and his officers in their decision to remain loyal : the effect was at once visible in the brightening of all faces. They also informed us that the fights at Abu Klea and Matammeh had produced a great effect on the Arabs, and that the Mahdi's emirs had declared they would not lead their men against the English again unless he accompanied them. One of these men was com-

missioned to go up to Khartum and find
out what had become of Khashm el Mus's
family.

Jan. 31*st*.—We commenced the descent
of the last narrow " gate " or passage of the
cataract, sending the nuggar on in front as
before.   We had to go down stern foremost, and had much difficulty in passing
the rocks on which we had grounded on
the 25th, for the current ran strong, and
the channel made a bend—very dangerous
for a steamer the length of the ' Bordein,'
at this stage of the water.   However, with
hawsers out and steaming ahead, we eventually got through, and then dropped down
the remainder of the cataract.

At 10 A.M., when we were out of the bad
water, we stopped for wood, of which we
were running very short, having used up
our reserve supply, and burnt all the ammunition - cases we could find empty.   I
intended taking in only enough to carry us

an hour beyond Wad Habashi, which we hoped to pass at full speed without being badly hulled; and I wanted to finish this second wooding before sunset, so as to get a little farther down and anchor in mid-stream. There was, however, no wood, except that of a couple of *sakiehs;* and it took us two hours to dismantle these, cut the poles to the required length, and carry the wood on board. Whilst this was going on, a few shots were fired at us without doing any harm. Before we started I had logs of wood, boxes of stores, &c., put over the boiler to protect it. Went round to see everything was ready for running past the batteries, and spoke again to the captains and *reises*, urging them to do their best when taking the ship past the enemy.

Just after we had started I was told that Abd ul Hamid had managed to send off a letter to some one by a native he had found on shore. I taxed him with

it, and of course he lied, swearing it was
to a friend in Khartum to inquire about
his family. I now had serious doubts of
his good faith, but did not see how he could
harm us, and thought that the large sums
I had promised the captains would induce
them to act loyally, as we were so nearly
out of danger.

Curiously enough, this was the only day
on which I had felt at all nervous as to the
result. I had been anxious enough on previous days, but always had a feeling we
should pull through. This day I seemed to
have a presentiment of coming evil. I had
been on deck nearly the whole morning,
and did not leave it until the captains
pointed out to me the low spit of Wad
Habashi, and said that the cataract was
finished, and there was open water until
we got to the passage in front of the battery. Then I went into the cabin to sit
down for a little before the fight. I had

not been there a quarter of an hour, and
we were congratulating ourselves on having
got down the cataract safely, and speculat-
ing on our chances of running past the battery without serious injury, when the 'Bordein' ran on a sunken rock with a crash
that shook us all; but she came off at
once, and we hoped that no great harm had
been done. I rushed out of the cabin to
the fore part of the ship, and on looking
down into the fore-hold, saw that the water
had already covered the bottom, and was
coming in with great force. I shouted to
Ibrahim to tell the captains to lay her alongside a sandspit close at hand, and then went
back to the cabin, where the others had remained, thinking we were all right. They
would hardly believe me when I said, " It
is all up; we are wrecked, and the ship is
sinking fast." But they speedily realised
the fact, and then began to work with a
will.

We were soon alongside the sandspit, which turned out to be the end of a small wooded islet about fifty yards from the larger island of Mernat. We at once examined the hole in the ship's side, but found it impossible to stop it or to lower the water, though for more than an hour we worked hard with the pump, and lines of men with buckets. The hole was, unfortunately, below the water-line, in a difficult place to get at, and the water was soon several feet above it. Whilst Gascoigne and I were looking after this, Trafford and Wortley were landing the guns, ammunition, stores, and men. Of course there was much disorder, but on the whole the blacks behaved well, except on board the nuggar. When the ship struck and was turned round suddenly, the nuggar got loose; but the men worked her up to the spit under the stern of the steamer, and then began rushing in to loot what they could, especially from

the cabin. Our servants, who were clear-
ing out our things, rather lost their heads;
for, instead of knocking the first nigger
down, they allowed themselves to be hus-
tled.   Directly I heard the row I ran down
to the spit, drew my pistol, and threatened
to shoot the next man who tried to enter.
This and a good deal of strong language
stopped the rush, and I got the nuggar to
sheer off a little from the ship.

At last we had landed men, guns, ammunition, and such stores as we could save,
and were glad to find we had not lost
much of our own kits, only provisions and
some small things that had been lying
about in the cabin. A curious incident happened just after the ship had struck.   One
of the black soldiers, a Shilluk nigger, seized
a child of four or five and flung it into the
river: whether it was some wild idea of
propitiating the river-god, or an act of tem-
porary insanity in the midst of danger, I

could never make out. The act was seen by some of the Sussex men, and the savage was at once made prisoner and tightly bound.

As soon as the stores were out, I sent Gascoigne over to Mernat island to see if he could find a suitable place for a zeribah, as the island we were on was small, and completely commanded by Mernat. I went over myself soon after, having previously sent Trafford to occupy the larger island with a picket of the Sussex. I found Mernat covered with long grass and scattered trees, and Gascoigne reported the island to be about three-quarters of a mile wide and several miles long. He had found a small hamlet in the centre occupied by a few women, who fled at his approach, and ran to the side nearest the right bank of the river, where there was evidently a boat for crossing the narrow passage of 300 yards between the island and the mainland. It was a miserable place for defence, and I decided to make a forced

march down the right bank by moonlight
with the Sussex and Sudanese soldiers, and
to send the nuggar down with the sailors
and a small guard.

It was now nearly sunset, and Wortley
came over for last orders. I had previously told him, before landing on Mernat,
to pick out the best boat and boat's crew
he could, and have everything ready to
start down the river for Gubat as soon as
it was dark. I had no time to write, for
the wreck had only occurred at 3.30, and
I had been hard at work during the two
hours which had since passed. I told
Wortley to explain the situation, the fall
of Khartum, the two wrecks, &c.; also to
say that I was going to march down, and to
ask that a steamer might be sent up to meet
and support us. Khashm el Mus and a number of his men had in the meantime been
crossed over to Mernat with the nuggar, as
I wished to remove them from the tempta-

tion to loot the stores piled in a confused
mass on the sandspit. Trafford and Gascoigne returned to the small island to get
the Sudanese together, whilst I and Ibrahim
remained on Mernat to get the Sudanese
there to move.

When the order was given to prepare to
start, we could get no one to move. The
officers were worse than useless, and in
spite of a little kurbashing, would or perhaps could not help us. The blacks had
lighted fires, and were cooking savoury
messes, from which nothing could tear
them. I saw at once that it would be near
midnight before we could reach the mainland and make a fair start; and that we
should the next morning be in a hostile
country, over twenty miles from Gubat.
Besides, the men appeared to have become
much demoralised by the events of the last
few days. They and their officers were in
a state of collapse, and I did not know how

far I could depend upon their loyalty. I decided, therefore, to remain where we were, and had just time to let Wortley know the change of plan before he started. He left at 6.45 P.M., with a crew of four English soldiers and eight natives, and rowed down until near Wad Habashi, when the men stopped rowing, and the boat floated past the battery. They were so near, that Wortley could hear the men discussing whether they saw a boat or not. Just then the moon rose. The enemy saw them, and fired three volleys ; but they were already below the battery, and in a few moments were out of danger. Gascoigne and Trafford saw the flashes in the darkness, but we did not know Wortley had passed safely till next afternoon. The men in the boat must have worked well ; for Wortley reached Gubat at 3 A.M. next day, or a little more than eight hours for near forty miles.

o

The arrangements for the night were as follows. I slept on Mernat with Khashm el Mus and the crew of the 'Talahawiyeh,' acting on a timely hint of Ibrahim's never to leave the old man alone for a moment, or give him a chance of bolting. I had with me Ibrahim, my servant, and a guard of one corporal and three men of the Sussex, so as to give one sentry to pace up and down in front of the place where I slept, and wake me up in case of any movement. Trafford and Gascoigne, with the remainder of the Sussex and the crew and men of the 'Bordein,' slept on the smaller island, and guarded the stores, guns, and ammunition. As the 'Bordein' showed some signs of slipping off the bank into deep water, they put a hawser round her mast, and made it fast to a stout stake on the island.

I lay awake for a long time thinking over the situation, which was now suffi-

ciently critical to cause anxiety. I knew
that the Shagiyeh were the most fickle of
all the Sudanese, and that there was a
party in favour of surrender to the Mahdi.
It was also clear, from what we had seen,
that the crews and soldiers, with their
officers, were little better than river pirates;
and that having been living the free-and-
easy life of such men, they were little amenable to discipline. I had noticed, however,
certain jealousies between the officers, and
on these I intended to trade. I also knew
that the Turks, Circassians, and Egyptians would remain loyal to save their own
necks, and that the slaves would follow
their masters.

The problem was Khashm el Mus.
Would he stand by us or not? If he did,
I felt certain of being able to hold out until
relief came; for I knew that every effort
would be made to succour us. I went over
the *pros* and *cons*, and at last came to the

conclusion that the Mahdi would never
forgive him for having handed over the
steamers to the English, and for his fidelity
to Gordon under great temptation, as shown
by the letters[1] the Mahdi and others had
sent to him. I determined to pin my faith
on Khashm, and then fell asleep.

Feb. 1st.—The first thing we did was to
move every one across to the larger island,
except a guard of twenty natives, which
was left on the smaller island to prevent
any of the enemy's riflemen landing and
annoying us. I then got hold of Khashm
el Mus, and pointed out to him that if he
deserted us and went over to the Mahdi he
would certainly lose his head; but that if
he remained with us he would get promotion, be well treated, and have a chance of
avenging the slaughter of his family at

---

[1] These letters were found on the steamer. A selection,
which includes a letter announcing the defeat of the
British at Abu Klea, is given in Appendix IX.

Khartum when we advanced to take the place, as we certainly should. I also told him relief would be sure to come as quickly as possible. The old man swore by many oaths that he would remain faithful, and that he would be as loyal to me as he had been to Gordon. We then laid out the zeribah, had the men placed in the positions they were to occupy, and told each detachment to make the portion of fence to its front.

The Nile had fallen very low, leaving a steep, almost inaccessible bank, from 25 to 30 feet high, along the top of which ran a thicket of low bush two or three yards wide, except at one spot, which was clear of bush, and where there was a steep but fairly easy descent to the river. Here we had landed, and a rude path was soon made by the men carrying up the guns and stores. The line of bush acted as a good screen from the enemy's riflemen on the left bank of the

river, and here I determined to zeribah,
striking a rough semicircle from the opening
as centre.

The distribution of the men had been the
subject of anxious thought the night before.
How to arrange so that the different detachments should counteract each other was the
question, and here I found Ibrahim's knowledge of the Sudanese invaluable. He had
proved his pluck at Abu Klea and Matammeh, and had shown himself so attached to
me that I felt sure he would be loyal under
all circumstances.

It was a curious position to be in,—to
have to control a lot of wild Sudanese,
some of whose loyalty was doubtful, through
an Egyptian who had fought against us at
Tel-el-Kebir and been the friend of Arabi.
He was a small man of curious appearance,
with large projecting eyes, a cool manner unusual in an oriental, and a per-
suasive tongue, coupled with a way of mak-

ing himself ubiquitous which was really

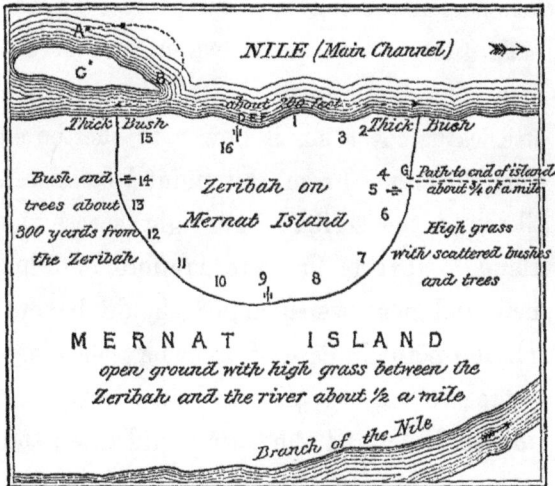

A. Rock on which the 'Bordein' struck, 31st January 1885.
B. Sandspit to which 'Bordein' was made fast. C. Small
wooded island. D. Landing and watering place. E. Station of
small boat. F. Station of large nuggar. G. Entrance to zeribah.
1. Headquarters: Sir C. Wilson and Khashm el Mus. 2. Captain
Trafford and detachment Royal Sussex Regiment. 3. Ammunition.
4. Shagiyeh of Khashm el Mus. 5. Gunners of 'Talahawiyeh.'
6. Mahdi Agha and Bashi Bazuks. 7. Sailors of 'Bordein.' 8. Ali
Agha and Bashi Bazuks. 9. Gunners of 'Talahawiyeh.' 10.
Shagiyeh of Abd ul Hamid. 11. Sailors of 'Talahawiyeh.' 12.
Captain Gascoigne, Bakhit Agha, and Sudan regulars. 13. Abd
ul Hamid and slaves. 14. Gunners of 'Bordein.' 15. Captains
and *reises.* 16. Abdullah Effendi and gunners of 'Bordein.'

remarkable. You will see the position by

the above sketch. I and Khashm, with
his personal following, were close to the
path going down to the water, and at the
foot of a large bush, in which the men
afterwards cut a small bower to shelter us
from the sun. From this point I could see
all round the zeribah and right across the
island. Next to us were Trafford and his
men, and here we arranged should be our
rallying-point in case of treachery—a place
where we might sell our lives dearly, or
whence, if we had time, we could reach the
boats. Next to the Sussex came a few
Shagiyeh of Khashm el Mus, and here we
made the entrance to the zeribah. A sentry
of the Sussex always paced from the gate to
the point where I was, so as to see every
one entering from the land side or coming
up from the water.

Next followed a gun with its gunners,
and then Mahdi Agha, a Mogrebin or Mor-
occo Arab, who I knew I could trust, with

his Bashi Bazuks. He had special orders
to watch the entrance and see that it was
closed at night. Next a lot of sailors, and
then Ali Agha, a fine soldierly Kurd, with
his Bashi Bazuks, who were really his own
slaves. Brave as a lion, he had unfortunately no head; but he was specially hated
by the Mahdists for some cruelties he had.
inflicted during the war. I therefore knew
he would fight to the last. Then came
a gun, the sailors of the 'Talahawiyeh,' the
Shagiyeh of Abd ul Hamid, and the black
Sudan regulars of Bakhit Agha.

Bakhit had in earlier days been one of Sir
Samuel Baker's "forty thieves," and he had
gradually worked his way up to the position
of captain of Sudan regulars. He was of
slave origin, and very proud of the position
he had won whilst eating the Khedive's
bread. It was almost certain that if taken
he would revert to his former position of
simple slave, and be sold to some Arab

taskmaster. He had everything to gain and nothing to lose by sticking to us, and I settled the matter by promising him promotion when we got down. I knew his men would follow him; but I was anxious about his lieutenant, a tall young black of excitable manner, who was related to Faraj Pasha, the man who betrayed Gordon and Khartum. Luckily he was very young, and had not much influence; but I had to watch him carefully, and was always anxious lest he should explode and bring on a crisis.

Next to Bakhit came Abd ul Hamid and his slaves; and Gascoigne slept close to the former, so as to keep a watch on Abd ul Hamid and that portion of the zeribah. Abd ul Hamid had thus to walk right in front of us to get out of the zeribah; but I trusted more to his attachment to a favourite slave girl, whom I thought, wrongly as it proved, he would not desert. With Abd ul Hamid was the Greek who had brought

down Gordon's last Journals with a favourable recommendation, but who, like that
spoiled child, was quite unworthy of Gordon's care. I had hoped he would be a
check on Abd ul Hamid, but I had reason
afterwards to suspect that he connived at
his escape, and was running double. He
wanted to escape with us, but he wished
to do something which, if we were lost,
would give him a claim to the Mahdi's
favour.

Next to Abd ul Hamid's slaves came a
gun, with its detachment; then the captains
and *reises*, with the remainder of the sailors;
and last, in a gun-pit facing the opening
towards the river, the fourth gun, under
Abdullah Effendi. Abdullah was a Saidi,
or fellah of Upper Egypt, who had been
some years in the Sudan. I had been
much taken by the way in which he had
worked his gun in the turret during the
action off Omdurman, and by his love of his

guns and devotion to his profession. He,
too, would lose his head if the Mahdi caught
him, so I felt certain of him and his black
slave gunners; for it is curious how the
slaves follow their officers, and the rude
idea of loyalty they have in not turning
against the Khedive, whose bread they eat.
Individuals may be treacherous, but not a
number of them.

I was very suspicious of the captains
and *reises*, who were nearly all Dongolese,
and therefore tribesmen of the Mahdi; and
not only certain to be well treated, but
rewarded and given employment if they
went over. To control them I trusted to
Captain Hamid Effendi, a one-eyed man,
a Saidi from Upper Egypt. He was really
captain of the 'Mansurah,' one of Gordon's
steamers which had been sunk off Shendy,
and should not have been with us, but he
had managed to stow himself away when
we started from Gubat. He had come to

the front very much on the voyage, especially when the 'Bordein' first ran aground
on the 25th; and in all our little accidents
afterwards he had been ever ready to volunteer for hard work, whether it was laying
out an anchor in the swift stream or pulling
on a hawser. When others had to be forced
to work, he was always ready to lend a hand
of his own free will. To him surrender to
the Mahdi was certain death.

I could thus depend upon more than
half the natives to stand by me, and
they, with the Sussex, were quite sufficient to resist any attack made upon
us whilst on the island; at any rate, we
were perfectly safe as long as Khashm el
Mus did not openly go over. The question
was whether, if we attempted to march
down by the right bank, these different
elements would hold together. The nuggar
and the remaining small boat were tied up
at the foot of the landing-place, and at

night one of the Sussex men was placed on
the former to prevent any attempt to cast
the boats adrift.   During the daytime we
kept up communication with the guard on
the islet with the small boat, always sending
a European with her.

The Sudanese worked capitally at the
zeribah, cutting and carrying in large
branches of the thorny mimosa, which
were interlaced in such a way as to present an impenetrable obstacle to a sudden
rush of the enemy ; then they made a shallow ditch on the inside of the hedge, just
wide enough for a man to lie down in.
They were careful to explain to me that they
never put anything in the centre of the
zeribah, as that was the most dangerous
place ; for all shots missing the hedge of
mimosa went just over it into the centre
of the zeribah.   Whilst the work was going
on, I called the superior officers to me one
by one, told them relief would be up in a

couple of days, praised their valour, &c.,
and promised them promotion when we
got down. I also discussed with them the
feasibility of a march down the right bank.
They all agreed that it would be practicable
if Khashm el Mus went with us, as his great
influence amongst the Shagiyeh would keep
them quiet, and he was much feared by the
Jalin, who made up the rest of the popula-
tion on that side.

When the zeribah was finished I called
the men to arms, to see whether each man
knew his proper place. It was a strange,
wild sight, as the Sudanese carry spears
instead of bayonets, finding the latter useless in fight with spearmen. I went round
with Khasm el Mus, whom I had previously
told to make a speech to each group of men.
The old man did it very well, and at one or
two places got quite eloquent in his exhorta-
tions and vigorous abuse of the Mahdi. It
had a good effect on the men, who answered

with the usual cries. Afterwards I called the officers together, and made them a speech. I was glad to see they took a less gloomy view of the situation than they had done on the previous evening: the excitement making the zeribah had caused them to forget their immediate troubles.

In my inspection of the zeribah, when I came to the part opposite Abd ul Hamid I found that he had bulged it out so as to include a shady bush under which he could lie down, and had made the hedge so loose that any one could walk through it with ease. I was very angry, the more so as Abd ul Hamid had been sulking all morning with his female slaves, and had not even been to say "good morning" to me. I rated him well, turned him out of his place, and got Bakhit Agha to draw the line in, and see that it was complete. In the evening, when I went round again, it was as strong as any other portion. We then

set the men to work to clear the grass inside and outside as a safeguard against fire.
They soon had the inside cleared up, the
Sudanese cutting the grass very rapidly
with their sharp knives; but outside did
not progress so quickly. The Sussex took
their turn at zeribah - making, but had
no proper tools for cutting, and were not
so handy as the Sudanese with their swords
and knives. They got their section into
very good order before nightfall.

Soon after the completion of the zeribah,
Khashm el Mus told me that some Shagiyeh,
one of whom was a relation of his, had
crossed to the island, and wished to speak
to him. I felt that I could not prevent communication between the men in the zeribah
and those outside, for they could not, for
sanitary reasons, be constantly confined to
the place, and the British force was too
small to establish an effective guard outside. I thought also that I should be more

P

likely to know what was really going on
if the communications were made under
my own eye and in Ibrahim's presence. I
therefore ordered them to be admitted, and
they came (four) in Mahdi's, or rather der-
vish dresses. They brought two curious
letters;[1] one promising Khashm el Mus
pardon if he surrendered, the other threat-
ening him with everlasting punishment if
he went down the river with us.

Khashm's relation, Sheikh Abulata, was
a fine-looking intelligent man, and spoke
quite openly about current events. He
told us that Wortley had passed the batteries in safety last night, so that we were
now certain he would reach Gubat, and it
was only a question of how long the steamers would take to get up, and whether they
would safely pass the battery, where, the
sheikh told us, there were two guns. They
confirmed the account of the fall of Khar-

:   [1] Appendix X.

tum, the death of Gordon, and the slaughter
of many Shagiyeh after the capture of the
town.   They openly proclaimed their intention of throwing in their lot with the
Mahdi now Khartum had fallen, and advised Khashm el Mus to do the same ; but
the old Bey refused, and said he intended
to stick to the English.   He told them to
look at the zeribah, and asked whether they
thought any force sent by the Mahdi could
take it ; then he added, the English will be
here to protect us in two days' time.   I
asked the Shagiyeh what they would do
if English troops came up ; to which they
replied that they would remain neutral.
Khashm el Mus then repeated that he knew
he was so compromised with the Mahdi
that he would not be spared if caught, and
that he would never surrender unless the
Mahdi sent him a letter under his own
seal formally promising him security and
protection.

I sent off two of Khashm el Mus's personal attendants to Halfiyeh to obtain news of Gordon and Khartum. After the Shagiyeh had gone, I sent Ibrahim and a couple of blacks to see how they had got across, and was delighted to hear that they had nothing but a *sampan*, or little boat, which only held four persons. Khashm also said that there were no larger boats below the cataract, as he had, by Gordon's order, destroyed them all. We could therefore only be attacked by a force landing by dribblets and collecting some distance off, and, with the bright moonlight, I had no fear of a surprise. When the men stood to their arms at sunset, it was reported that one of the black sailors had deserted—a trifling loss when it is considered that for a great part of the day the men had been much scattered cutting thorns for the zeribah hedge.

We had had a hard day's work in the

sun, but there was little real rest at night.
At sunset we surrounded the zeribah with
pickets of four men and a non-commissioned
officer, selected, as far as possible, to avoid
treachery ; but we could not get them to
go more than fifty yards in front of the zeribah. Gascoigne had charge of these pickets,
and went round them every two or three
hours during the night. Within the zeribah
we had a line of sentries, which Trafford
visited ; whilst I turned out twice to take a
look round in the bright moonlight. The
sentries were much more on the alert than
we expected, and the night passed quietly,
though we had fully anticipated an attack.
At dinner we had a long talk over the
situation, which now seemed less gloomy
than it did before.

Feb. 2d.—After I had made my morning
round of the zeribah, I went with Gascoigne
and one of the *reises* named Imam to examine the river at the end of the island, in

case we should have to cross to the right
bank and march down. We made our way
through long grass, and pretty, almost park-
like scenery, to the point, and found the
river narrow, but the entrance to the main
branch unfortunately so blocked by rocks
that it would be impossible to bring up the
nuggar to help in the crossing ; we should
therefore have to cross every one in the
small boat—a very long operation. There
was, however, a good landing-place of rock
on the opposite shore, then a palm-grove,
and behind that a small isolated rocky hill,
at the foot of which we were told the road
ran. It was clear that if we could once
seize this hill, we should be able to cross
the men without much loss. We could see
some villagers in the distance, but kept
behind bushes and were not observed.

On the way back we put up a large pack
of guinea-fowl, the first I had seen in
Africa, but Gascoigne told me they were

very plentiful farther south. When we got back we set men to work to caulk our small boat, which leaked badly, and also to make oars, for we had given Wortley all the oars except two broken ones, so as to let him have every chance of getting through. We got the wood from the 'Bordein,' and our men, aided by the native carpenters, managed to turn out four very fair oars.

The Shagiyeh came again to the zeribah and begged Khashm el Mus to go to the edge of the island to talk to his sister, who had come down from Halfiyeh, and some other Shagiyeh. I did not like this at first, but was now pretty certain of Khashm, and felt I could not throw away any chance of obtaining news of Gordon's fate; evidently we could hear nothing if we had no communication with the people. I considered our position in the zeribah with the four guns a very strong one, and I felt certain the steamers would arrive next

day. I therefore consented, on condition
that Bakhit Agha and Ibrahim were present at the interview. With Bakhit I sent
five regulars, who were to remain out of
earshot; and between them and the zeribah
I had a picket of Shagiyeh as a connect-
ing link. About 2 P.M. they returned to
the zeribah, and told us that a Shagiyeh
had come up the opposite bank with news
that the two steamers had left Gubat about
noon the previous day. Khashm el Mus's
sister had brought down the news that
Gordon was killed whilst coming out of his
room, the same story of the betrayal of the
town by Faraj Pasha, and that there had
been a massacre of the Shagiyeh, Turks,
Egyptians, and Europeans, during which
the families of the men with us had been
killed. There might be some survivors,
and Khashm asked me to give him some
money to enable his sister to try and obtain
their ransom. To this I agreed, and gave

him £110 to ransom such of his and Abd
ul Hamid's family as remained alive. I
also told him to tell his sister to come
down to us at Gubat with such additional
information as she could collect.

Khashm, Bakhit, and Ibrahim again went
out with the same precautions as before,
and returned about 5 P.M. with rather start-
ling news. First, on their getting to the
bank they found Feki Mustafa, who commanded the Mahdi's force at Wad Habashi,
there with three of his men. He tried
all he could to induce Khashm to desert
us; but the old man remained firm, and
said he would not go over to the Mahdi
until he received a safe-conduct from him.
Feki Mustafa had married the first cousin
of Khashm, so that the two men were connected by marriage, and knew each other
well. Ibrahim, who is a keen observer, told
me that he was certain Feki Mustafa was a
great coward; that he had seemed nervous

during the interview; and that he saw him
give a start when a random shot was fired
at the zeribah from the opposite bank.
One of the women had whispered to Ibrahim that he was not to be afraid, as the
English were on their way up; and he had
heard Khashm el Mus's sister tell him that
he was on no account to surrender, as the
Mahdi had determined to kill him.   He
found out that Feki Mustafa intended to
come to the island next day, and make
another attempt on Khashm's loyalty.
Ibrahim also brought the news that whilst
they were talking Abd ul Hamid Bey and
Imam the *reis*, who had been out with
us in the morning, had deserted with the
whole of the Shagiyeh picket.   This was
serious news, and created much excitement
amongst the natives in the zeribah.   How
Abd ul Hamid and Imam managed to slip
out without our noticing them I never
quite knew; but I found out afterwards

that the Greek was aware beforehand of
his intention to desert, and I strongly suspect he connived at his escape.

I was a good deal put out at this news;
but it was necessary to put a bold face on
the matter, so I arrested the remaining captains and *reises*, and placed them under a
guard of the Sussex, with orders that they
were to be shot if they attempted to escape.
I then called the native officers together,
told them we were well rid of a man like
Abd ul Hamid, who was more dangerous to
us inside the zeribah than outside, where
he could do nothing; that the steamers
were sure to arrive next day, and that
we should then all go down the river together. The men were next called to arms,
and I made old Khashm go round with me
and address the natives as he had done before. He spoke really well, having worked
himself up into a state of excitement, and
his speech produced a good effect.

Abd ul Hamid's slave girl was in a great
state at being deserted by her master, and
evidently knew nothing of his intention to
desert. He was one of the many instances
in which Gordon's trust in natives was
misplaced. I never understood Gordon's
policy with natives. No one knew better
how false and treacherous they are, and yet
he used to trust them on occasions in the
most implicit way, and was constantly
being taken in. Muhammed el Kheir is
another instance. He had been loaded
with favours by Gordon, and at one time
received an annuity from him; yet he went
over to the enemy at once, and is now Emir
of Berber for the Mahdi.

Abd ul Hamid appears to have been
treated by Gordon like a spoiled child, and
he had been well treated by us on all occasions; yet he could not bear the restraints
of the zeribah, and thought he could do
better for himself by going over to the

Mahdi. I fancy that even Khashm el Mus
was more influenced by his personal fears,
and the ill treatment which his cousin Saleh
Wad el Mek had received at the hands of
the Mahdi, than by any love for the English or respect for Gordon; yet it must
always stand to his credit that he did remain loyal throughout under much temptation. Ever since the wreck, Abd ul Hamid
had sulked amongst his slaves, and I was
always rather suspicious of him; but after
we received the news that the steamers were
coming to our relief, I never thought he
would bolt as he did. The truth is, I fancy,
that the fall of Khartum and the subse-
quent massacres had completely thrown the
natives off their balance; they seemed to
have quite lost their heads.

At night the natives refused to go outside the zeribah as they had done on the
previous night, so we had to be content
with a strong line of sentries inside, which

was constantly visited by Trafford and Gascoigne during the night : they always found
the sentries well on the alert.   It had been
an anxious day, as we never knew what
was going to happen, and we had to watch
our natives much as a cat does a mouse.

At dinner we discussed our chances of
escape. We felt certain the steamers would
come; but then there was just a chance
they would not, and the possibility of
their being disabled by the batteries. We
also talked over our chances of getting
down by the right bank, and determined
to attempt it if no relief came next day.
The difficult point was with regard to the
wounded ; and we came to the conclusion
that if any Englishman was too badly
wounded to march, he would have to be
shot to prevent his falling into the enemy's
hands.   On one point we were all agreed,
that we would never surrender, but sell our
lives as dearly as we could.   I must not

forget one point about the zeribah: it was
the worst place for white ants I was ever
in; they attacked blankets and everything.

Feb. 3d.—We had expected an attack last
night; but the evening passed off quietly,
and the enemy lost their chance when the
moon rose about 10 P.M. Before going to
sleep last night, I made up my mind to seize
Feki Mustafa when he came to the island,
and to hold him a hostage for our safety
during the march down the right bank,
which I intended to commence at mid-day
if the steamers did not appear by that time.
Just as it was getting daylight, I ordered
the troops to be confined to the zeribah, and
then arranged for the seizure of Feki Mustafa by Ibrahim, Bakhit Agha, and some of
his regulars, as soon as he set foot on the
island. As I was arranging this matter,
Gascoigne reported to me that Khashm el
Mus had gone outside the zeribah with three
or four men. I was much annoyed, and

Gascoigne and I went out with some men to
watch him. He returned in a few minutes,
and was indignant at what he called our
doubts of his loyalty. I told him we had
no doubt of that, but that an order having been given for no one to leave the
zeribah, he should have been the last man
to break it. The old man was in an
excitable state, and I returned with him
to our place in the zeribah, whilst Trafford
and Gascoigne went to the end of the
island to watch for the steamer. I noticed
in passing that the blacks were a good deal
excited : evidently they realised, as we did,
that a crisis was approaching ; so I did all I
could to quiet down Khashm, and sent Ali
and Mahdi Aghas to keep the men quiet.

As I was talking to Khashm, we suddenly heard the report of a gun down-
stream, and the effect was electrical. There
was a general shout of "Ingliz! Ingliz!" and
every one's spirits rose a hundred per cent.

I sent a man up a high tree close to the
place where we slept, who reported that he
could see the steamer—he was not sure
whether there was one or two—keeping up
a fire on the fort. I was listening to the
cannonade, rather surprised at its long
continuance, when Gascoigne came running
back to report, and crossed over to the small
island to hoist the flags on the 'Bordein'
so as to show our exact position; and I had
the gun pointing towards the river loaded
to fire the three shots agreed upon with
Wortley to show we were all right. As
it turned out, the relieving party were so
busily engaged themselves they never saw
the flags or heard our guns.

As soon as the enemy on the left bank
saw the flags run up, they opened fire upon
us; and we replied with our Remingtons,
and shell from the gun. The blacks soon
began to get cheery: there seems to be
something in the sound of firing that pleases

Q

them. A few moments after, Trafford came in and reported that he had seen the steamer enveloped in smoke, and feared she had met with a serious accident. Gascoigne now returned, and took his station on the tree, and I went to have a look myself from the bank, whence I could see the steamer swinging at anchor and keeping up her fire on the battery.

We could not make out what had happened, and thought that one steamer had been crippled, and that the other had anchored to engage the battery and draw off the fire from her consort. I determined to break up the zeribah at once and march down the right bank, so as to effect a junction with the force on the steamers, feeling sure that, whatever had occurred, our united forces would be more than a match for any enemy we might meet.

I told Khashm el Mus we must go down to the steamers, and then ordered the zeribah to be broken up. As soon as the order was given, a scene of wild confusion arose. It became impossible to keep the wild Sudanese under control. Every man tried to save his little bit of private property, and all made a rush for the nuggar. I sent the Sussex men down to the nuggar to prevent their overloading her ; and they worked hard, but they were too few to stand against the rush, and much useless lumber was put on board. Whilst the Sussex were doing this and stowing the ammunition, dura, &c., at the bottom of the nuggar, their kits, which had been left on the bank, were looted by some of the blacks. To add to the confusion, the enemy opened a sharp fire on us, and several men were hit as they were scrambling up and down the banks. Some of our deserters were evidently with them, for a heavy fire was kept up the whole time on the place where Khashm and I had slept.

At last guns, ammunition, and stores
were on board, and the Sudanese became
quite quiet, and collected together for the
march. On the nuggar, besides the stores,
were the wounded, some sailors, a small
guard of the Sussex, and about fifty Bashi
Bazuks ; also our servants and baggage.
I placed Gascoigne in command of the
nuggar, and told him to float down and
stop on the right bank as near the end of
the island as possible, until we joined him.
The felucca or small boat was sent down at
the same time, with orders to meet us at
the end of the island.

The remainder of the Sussex under Trafford then formed up on the island ; and as
they were doing this, one of them had a
lucky escape. I heard a " thud " close beside me, and a man shout " Oh ! " and
turned round just in time to see him fall.
I asked, " Where is he hit ? " and the
reply was, " In the foot, sir." But when

we came to examine, we found the ball had
gone in and out of his boot, making two
holes, without breaking the skin. The
shock had knocked him off his legs; but
he was able to hobble along, and the effect
of the blow gradually wore off.

We now marched down to the end of
the island, congratulating ourselves that we
had started without any enemy having
attempted to land and molest us whilst
breaking up the zeribah. On reaching the

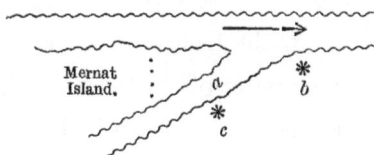

end of the island we met the small boat, and
at once began to cross over. We first lined
the bank at *a* with the Sussex to cover the
landing, and then stretched a line of black
sentries across the island. When this was
done, I sent Ali Agha across with a dozen

Bashi Bazuks to take possession of the little hill *c*. No one opposed the landing; but directly the Bashi Bazuks got into the bush they began firing—I heard afterwards they saw one man and missed him—and I soon saw them on the hill *c*. After the third boat-load had crossed, Gascoigne came up with the good news that he had occupied a little hill, *b*, about half a mile lower down on the right bank, with his Bashi Bazuks, and had seen no enemy. The Sussex were now crossed over, and I followed them with Khashm el Mus; then came the remainder of the blacks; the rear-guard being Bakhit Agha and his regulars.

It took a long time to cross with the one small boat, but we finally got over, and the boat was sent down to join the nuggar. There was only one accident,—a man's rifle went off and shot another in the back, but not badly. We met here the messenger I had sent down by land with

a note to Boscawen in case Wortley did
not get through. He told us that when
approaching Gandattu he had seen the
steamers coming up, and then returned.
He insisted that there were two steamers,
so we were now afraid one of them had
been sunk by the battery. It turned out
to be a curious instance of native exag-
geration.[1]

When we had effected a junction with
Gascoigne and the nuggar, I told him to
float down to a point on the right bank
opposite the ' Es Safia,' as we now saw the
steamer to be, whilst we marched for the
same place. We could plainly see the
fight going on, and as we got nearer could
make out the white ensign flying bravely in
the breeze, a pleasant sight for hard-pressed
Britishers. We marched down through a

[1] It was only after Captain Gascoigne had been on
board the ' Es Safia,' and communicated with Lord Charles
Beresford, that we knew that only one steamer had come
up, and that the native report was wrong.

pretty and richly cultivated country, with
much Indian corn just ripe, and reached
the bank opposite the 'Es Safia,' at a
sakieh, where we established ourselves.

On our way we saw several horsemen,
but they all beat a speedy retreat before
the fire of the blacks, whom I had sent out
as skirmishers to cover our right flank.
The blacks set fire to everything *en route*
that would burn, but that was only a few
mat and straw huts.   When we got opposite the steamer, we could see that she was
anchored, and that her machinery or boiler
must be damaged.   The steamer now began
to signal to us, and after some time we
made out the message to mean that she was
hit in the boiler, but that they could mend
it during the afternoon and night, and
would pick us up next morning if we went
lower down to a place where the water was
deep close to the bank, and "zeribahed"
ourselves there for the night.

Whilst the signalling was going on, we had something to eat, which we were glad to get, after our long morning's work and three-mile march down the bank, for our breakfast had been put an end to by the break-up of the zeribah.   We got one of the guns from the nuggar, and Abdullah Effendi and his blacks soon brought it into action against the centre embrasure of the enemy's battery.   I also placed a lot of blacks along the bank, and had four of the best marksmen of the Sussex on the sand near the water's edge : they lay down and made excellent practice at 1100 yards. We could see the bullets striking the parapet and the sides of the embrasures.

As we had no good signaller with us, and communication with the steamer was difficult, Gascoigne volunteered to go over to her in our small boat.   I sent the two naval artificers with him and a native crew. Gascoigne's boat was received with a hot but

badly directed fire, and he managed to go
and return without having a man hit.   He
told us they were all well and cheery on
board, and had lost one officer wounded,
a seaman killed, and several men badly
scalded by the rush of steam out of the
boiler.   The boiler would be mended by
sunset, and Beresford wished us to keep
up our fire till dark, so as to take off
the enemy's attention from his steamer.
Unfortunately we had only saved enough
ammunition for one gun, and even some
of that was damp, so that the shells did
not burst as well as they ought to have
done.   Abdullah Effendi made, however,
on the whole very fair practice; and two
or three of our shells burst in the battery.
The enemy replied to us with solid shot,
but not with much spirit, and their shot
went screaming over our heads.   Their rifle-
fire was also somewhat wild, and the bullets
fell fifty or sixty yards behind us.

Between us and the battery there was a long sandbank; and the *reis* having said there was a passage near the right bank on which we were, Gascoigne tried to get down it, but the nuggar grounded, and he had to land every one except the badly wounded. The enemy of course opened fire on him; but all the shots were too high or too low. As it was now getting late in the afternoon, I sent Trafford and the Sussex on with Khashm el Mus and most of his men to select a place where Beresford could pick us up, and make a zeribah for the night, whilst I remained with the gun and about thirty men to attract the fire of the enemy from the nuggar.

It was nearly sunset when we saw the nuggar afloat again; and then, as we could be of no further use, we commenced our march through the tangled vegetation, beans, Indian corn, dura, &c. As we got on, the men dragging the gun became quite exhausted ; and even Abdullah, whose love for his piece was quite touching, had to acknowledge they could not get it any farther.   I then gave orders that it was to be spiked and thrown into the river—the gun in one place, and the different parts of the carriage in others.   After this was done we went on to the zeribah, which we reached after dark.   It was not a very lively outlook, as we had no blankets and no food, all our things being in the nuggar.   However, Khashm el Mus's men had collected a lot of corn-cobs, and caught some goats, which were soon killed and grilling before the camp-fire.

Soon after we got in, we were surprised at the arrival of the small boat with a number of women, a few men, and Private Paine of the Sussex, who told us that the boat had left Gascoigne without permission, and that he wanted her back again.   I got

a native crew into the boat, and sent Paine
up by land to tell Gascoigne she was coming; he took with him three natives, sailors,
to help. The boat came back after about
three-quarters of an hour — the boatmen
saying it was quite impossible to get up-
stream with the strong wind which had
sprung up since sunset. In about two
hours Paine returned, and said the nuggar
had changed her position, and he thought
she must be on a rock in the middle of the
river. I then manned the boat again with
two Sussex men and two native sailors.
They were out for two hours pulling
against the stream; but the wind was so
high they could make no progress, and so
came back.

About 1.30 or 2 A.M. one of Gascoigne's
sailors came down. He had swum from
the nuggar to the right bank, and then
made his way through the bush to our
camp. He told us that the nuggar was

aground on a rock close under the battery, and in front of the centre embrasure, and that it was impossible to
get her off without the small boat to lay
out anchors. It appears that Gascoigne,
finding the boat did not return, started
off in the nuggar, hoping to be able to
float past the battery before the moon
rose; but just as they thought they were
safe, she grounded firmly on a couple
of rocks, and no exertions could get her
off.

We started the boat again, and luckily
this time successfully; for the wind fell
before morning, and she reached Gascoigne
as the first streak of dawn was appear-
ing. We were very thankful to have got
thus far in safety, and our only anxiety
now was lest a stray shot should hit the
steamer coming down ; or worse, if the
enemy had only the wit to withdraw one
of their guns, take it up the bank opposite

the steamer, and open fire on her when the moon rose.

The night passed in perfect quietness, except for the tom-toming which we heard occasionally in the distance. It was bitterly cold at our zeribah in spite of the large fires we kept up. We scraped hollows in the ground; but there was no escape from the bitter cold wind, which found us out everywhere. I hardly slept the whole night, and I do not think any of the natives did. It was bad enough for us with our thin *khaki* clothes; so what it must have been for natives, with nothing but a white cotton dress on, may be imagined. Without proper night-covering these cold nights are very trying, especially to Englishmen with not very much inside them.

Feb. 4th.—As daylight approached the wind fell, but it was still bitterly cold, and there was little to warm us in our frugal breakfast of " corn-cobs " and Nile water.

All eyes were turned towards Wad Habashi,
and the increasing light had just enabled us
to distinguish the steamer and nuggar when
we heard the first shot fired. For a few
minutes the firing was continuous, and we
could distinctly hear above all the sharp
grunt of the Gardner; then we saw the
little steamer run past the nuggar and
bring up in mid-stream, still keeping up
her fire on the battery. After a few moments' suspense we could see a boat leave
the steamer for the nuggar, and I at once
sent Bakhit Agha, with his regulars and
some of the Bashi Bazuks, up the river to
divert the attention of the enemy, and, if
possible, render assistance. At last the
nuggar got off the rocks and was taken in
tow by the steamer. When they came opposite the zeribah we were asked to go about
a mile lower down, where there was a better
place for embarking; so we marched for the
rendezvous, and reached it without opposi-

tion. I was glad to find Gascoigne and his small party had escaped without a scratch. They had been aground within about 400 yards of the fort, and the Arabs had done their best to sink them. Luckily, though the nuggar was repeatedly hit by rifle-bullets, all the shot and shell either went over their heads or struck the water in front of them; and the only man touched was Keppel, R.N., commanding the blue-jackets sent to Gascoigne's assistance, who was struck by a spent ball, but not injured. The coolness shown by Gascoigne and his men in their trying position, and also by Keppel and his sailors who assisted him in lightening the nuggar and getting her off the rocks, is beyond all praise. Curiously enough, though the nuggar was only about 500 yards from the steamer, and there was bright moonlight after midnight, no one saw her until the steamer ran past her in the morning. I suppose she must have been in line with

R

the bank, and so not noticed by the "look-out" man on the 'Es Safia.' I was again unlucky, for my servant, who had been sent in the nuggar to look after the baggage, allowed half my small kit to be thrown overboard; and all my private cash, and many things not to be replaced out here, now lie at the bottom of the Nile. Fortunately a box of silver dollars, which I was taking to Khartum, was saved. It had been built into the zeribah walls at Abu Klea and Gubat, been wrecked in the 'Bordein' and landed on Mernat island, yet it came down to Gubat without the loss of a dollar. On the steamer we met Wortley, who had had the unique experience of having been wrecked three times in one week. It appears that every one on the steamer was so busily engaged that they never heard our firing in the morning, or saw the flags we had hoisted on the 'Bordein.' We heard many details of Beresford's plucky up-hill fight with the battery. The little steamer had almost passed when her boiler was struck, and she went on for about 200 yards before the engine stopped; then she anchored. The Gardner and one of the small guns were at once brought to bear on the battery, and kept up throughout the day such a continuous well-aimed fire that the Arabs could never use their up-stream gun with any effect, or show their heads above the parapet. The boiler was mended, under circumstances of great difficulty, by Mr Benbow, Chief Engineer, who had fortunately reached Gubat with the 2d Division of the Naval Brigade whilst we were up the river. The two officers who were with Beresford—Van Koughnet, who was wounded, and Keppel—came across at the same time, and so did Bower, who commanded the Mounted Infantry on board. The enemy must have been rather demoralised by the day's fighting, for they never

made any attempt to remove one of the
guns from the battery and run it up to a
point on the bank opposite the steamer.
They might have done this easily and have
sunk the steamer; but they possibly looked
upon her as a sure prize, and expected to
find her deserted in the morning. I was
told that when they saw the 'Es Safia'
getting up steam in the morning, they
uttered a most peculiar yell of mingled rage
and disappointment. On our way down
we were fired at from a few places on the
left bank, and once we struck heavily on a
sandbank in mid-stream, but we were soon
off again without damage. Wortley brought
up a budget of home letters, which were
very acceptable after the hard work of the
last fortnight. We stopped once to take in
wood, and reached Gubat about 5.30 P.M.
I found Boscawen and Verner laid up with
fever, and Willson, Scots Guards, in command; and was surprised to learn that they

had received no communication of any kind
from headquarters, and that the only reinforcements which had arrived were the
2d Division of the Naval Brigade and the
second half-battery of artillery. All the
available camels had been sent to Jakdul
on the 1st, to wait for the reinforcements
which every one expected were now on
their way to Gubat. The position was un-
changed, except that forage for the camels
and horses was getting scarce in the immediate vicinity of the camp. I slept on the
' Es Safia,' where Beresford kindly gave me
a bed, and felt thankful that we had got so
well out of the difficulty caused by the loss
of both the steamers. Beresford had appeared in the ' Es Safia ' off Wad Habashi
almost at the very hour the natives had led
us to expect him; and though the accident
to the boiler prevented his coming to the
island some three miles higher up the river,
his presence and his gallant action with the

battery enabled us to cross from the island to the mainland without opposition, and retire in safety. It is creditable to the natives that not one of them deserted on the march down, though they knew the steamer was in difficulties, and might not be able to help us when we reached her.

Feb. 5th.—A Court of Inquiry was assembled, under Beresford's presidency, to examine into the circumstances under which the two steamers were lost, and into the conduct of the captains and *reises.* When the ' Talahawiyeh ' was wrecked, Trafford and Wortley were of opinion that it was an accident; and the great care shown by the captains in bringing the ' Bordein ' down the cataract confirmed us in this view, until the second wreck occurred. We then had great reason to believe that both boats had been lost by treachery; but we could not understand why the captains had wrecked the ' Bordein ' below the cataract, when in less than an hour she would have been below Wad Habashi. There was little evidence of value; but, under the peculiar circumstances, it was decided to send them before a court-martial next day.[1] During the course of the day we paraded the natives, and had them counted, and their names written down with their rank. It was a tedious, troublesome piece of work, but not without some amusing incidents; and the appearance of the various groups under their several leaders was very quaint.

[1] I cannot now help thinking that both the wrecks were accidental, due partly to carelessness and partly to the low state of the river. From Wad Habashi to Jebel Royan the river is dangerous from the number of sunken rocks, and it was unusual to take boats of the size of the 'Bordein' down the cataract at that time of year. It must be remembered, too, that the turrets and armour made the steamers draw much more water than usual, and the captains may not have made allowance for this. The steamer upon which I came down the river from Assuan to Siut ran aground seven or eight times, and in nearly every case the accident was due to inattention on the part of the *reis*, or to the helmsman's having mistaken the direction given to him.

Two or three of the officers had managed
to save their blue coats from the wrecks;
but most of the men were in very tattered
apparel, and some had nothing but a long
cotton shirt and the belt in which they
carried their cartridges. The sergeant, who
spoke Italian, and who had surrendered at
Abu Klea, was still in his Mahdi uniform,
and looked as comical as ever. When
going up the river I had handed him over
to Bakhit Agha, and he turned out to be one
of our best shots. He had always a broad
grin on his black face, and fought against
the Mahdi's men as stoutly as he had done
against us at Abu Klea. Abdullah, the
gunner captain, was sent with his guns
into the fort; the others camped outside,
and were placed in Gascoigne's charge. I
was glad to get my ulster again, which
Verner had fortunately recovered whilst I
was up the river; but my camels had gone
off with the convoy to Jakdul, and I had to

get one for the journey across the desert,
which I wished to make quickly, so as to
relieve the anxiety which I knew must be
felt with regard to the safety of the ship-
wrecked party.   Trafford and Gascoigne
remained at Gubat, whilst Wortley and I
went up at sunset to the Guards' redoubt
at Abu Kru, whence we were to start for
Korti.

To my great regret, I had to leave Gubat
without seeing Stewart.   His wound appeared to be going on favourably, but he
had a feverish attack, and it was feared
that the excitement of talking about Khartum and Gordon with me would do him
harm : no one seemed then to expect a fatal
result.   Stewart was not only a thorough
soldier, but a first-rate man of business, and
this enabled him to get through an amount
of work which would have tried most men,
with apparent ease.   He was a charming
companion, kind and courteous to those

who served under him, and beloved by all
ranks.   A more gallant officer never lived,
and his death was mourned for as that of a
personal friend by every one in the desert
column.   What an ill-fated expedition this
has been!   The whole Sudan is not worth
the lives of men like Gordon and the two
Stewarts.

Feb. 6th.—After the moon had risen, an
escort from the Guards' Camel Regiment,
under Vesey Dawson, formed up in a little
hollow beneath the redoubt, and at 1.30
A.M. we started.   For two hours we travelled a little west of north, then we
changed our direction to a little east of
north, and shortly after daybreak we struck
the road from Matammeh to Abu Klea.
We must have passed close to the wells of
Shebacat, as we crossed a large open space
which had been much used as a camping-
ground; but we saw no one, and being a
small party, found no difficulty in passing

through the belt of wood which had thrown
the convoy into such disorder during the
night - march of the 18th - 19th January.
We reached Abu Klea at 9 A.M., having
made the journey in only 7½ hours. The
Sussex detachment left to guard the wells
had greatly strengthened the small work
they were living in, and had much improved the wells; but I was sorry to hear
the water was not running into some of
them as freely as it had done. St Vincent and Lyall, R.A., had died of their
wounds; the other wounded had been sent
back to Jakdul, and were reported to be
doing well. The small garrison had never
been molested by the Arabs; but after
receipt of the news of the fall of Khartum, it had been strengthened by a detachment of the Heavies under Davison.
We left the wells at 11.45 A.M., and reached
the zeribah in which we had passed the
night of the 16th-17th at 1 P.M.; the dis-

tance is therefore about 3½ miles. The
battle-field was a horrible sight; for though
many of the Arabs had been buried, numbers were still lying about, and the large
heaps of slain in front of the square had
not been touched. In a little hollow on the
farther side of the valley I noticed the body
of a poor child of five or six, who had been
struck by a random shot. Death must have
been instantaneous, for the body looked as
if the child had fallen asleep. Davison
and his men had erected a large cairn over
the grave of their comrades, and the Arabs
had marked the last resting-places of their
principal men. The Sussex officers told me
that several days after the battle they had
found wounded men in the long grass in the
valley, who had been kept alive by water
and food brought to them during the
night from Matammeh. As soon as we had
got well clear of the Abu Klea hills, we
halted for a short rest, and then kept on

till sunset, when we camped a short distance to the east of Jebel Sergain.   We saw
no one but two men and a camel in the far
distance; but Wortley was lucky enough to
secure a gazelle, which was a welcome addition to the "bully" beef.

Feb. 7th.—We left about an hour before
daybreak, and reached Jakdul about two
hours before sunset.   We met no one on
the road until we had left the sandy district and were ascending the long slope to
Jakdul; there we overtook the cook of the
18th Royal Irish Regiment and some other
men returning to Jakdul.   They told us
that the regiment had left Jakdul on foot
before daylight, and that they had accompanied it for some distance, when they had
been left behind to load up some firewood
which was found near the road.   When they
started again the regiment was out of sight,
and they had travelled well on into the day
without seeing any trace of it.   As we had

seen no one on the road, we were rather
anxious about the regiment until we reached
Jakdul, and heard that Lord Cochrane, who
knows the country well, had gone with it
as guide.   The 18th had marched on foot
from Korti, and made very good time to
Jakdul, where they arrived in splendid
condition, without, I ·believe, a single man
falling out.   They completed the march to
Gubat without difficulty, and one cannot
help regretting that one or two of the regiments which went up the river with Earle
were not sent across in the same way.   As
we approached Jakdul we met a convoy on
its way to Gubat, and at Jakdul itself we
found Buller, who had been appointed to
the command of the desert column when
the news of Stewart's wound reached Korti.
Kitchener had come with him, and, I was
glad to find, was to go on to Gubat.   Buller
hoped to be able to take Matammeh when
he got to Gubat ; but the future of the cam-

paign was doubtful, as no indication had come of the policy which would be adopted when the news of the fall of Khartum reached England. I think the general impression was that Government would say that Khartum having fallen, the object of the expedition was at an end, and that they would revert to the policy of having nothing to do with the Sudan. The capture and burning of Matammeh, and then a withdrawal to Wady Halfa, seemed to many of us the most likely programme. The Sussex had greatly improved Jakdul by removing the loose stones and making roads for some distance outside of the crater, or inner basin; but the camping-ground itself was becoming rather unpleasant from the number of men and camels that had stopped there on various occasions. I was very glad to find Dickson's wound going on well, and all the wounded sent back from Abu Klea appear to have stood the journey well.

Feb. 8th.—We started early for Howeiyat, leaving Vesey Dawson and the escort
to return to Gubat with Buller, who was
going to leave a little later.   We were
accompanied at first by Mr Pearse of the
'Daily News,' and Mr Villiers of the ' Graphic'; but Mr Villiers's camel going slowly,
we gradually got a long way ahead of the
two correspondents, who kept together.
Near Abu Halfa we met a large convoy
under Stanley Clarke, who was carrying a
mail to the front, which he very kindly
opened to give me my letters—a rare treat
in the desert.   After passing the curious
hill of Zobrik el Kelb, Ibrahim, I, and
Wortley's servant inadvertently took the
road near the hills which Stewart had followed when he first went to Jakdul; whilst
Wortley, who had been trotting on ahead,
took the lower road by which we had travelled on the second advance to Jakdul.
We got to Howeiyat a little after sunset,

and found Wortley had arrived a few minutes before us.   The upper road leads into
the broad valley in which the wells are
situated, two or three miles above them;
and it is rather difficult to find, as there
are many tracks and a good deal of high
grass and bush.   We were anxious about
Mr Pearse and Mr Villiers, as they did not
come in, though we had a large bonfire
lighted as a beacon on a hill above the
camp.   The detachment of the Essex, under
Captain Carter, had deepened the wells and
got the station into capital order; but the
water-supply was diminishing, and giving
unpleasant symptoms of failing altogether.

Feb. 9th.—At dawn Carter sent out a
man to look for the two correspondents,
and we started on our long ride to Korti.
The man never met Messrs Pearse and
Villiers; and we heard afterwards that they
had followed the upper road, and reached

s

the valley where the road passed through the long grass, after dark. They had passed the night there without seeing our bonfire; and next morning, not recognising any features they knew, as they had come out by the lower road, they retraced their steps until they met a return convoy, with which they came on to Howeiyat. Our ride to Korti was uneventful; we travelled at the rate of a little over five miles an hour, and rode into camp as the rich afterglow was dying out from the sky. We had crossed the desert, a distance of 175 miles, in four days, and on the last day had ridden nearly 60 miles. I was very stiff when I got off my camel; but it was some recompense for the hard ride to know that the same evening all at home would know the ship-wrecked party had been rescued.

On the 11th, two days after my return

to Korti, the following telegram was placed in my hands :—

"War Secretary to Lord Wolseley.

"Express warm recognition of Government of brilliant services of Sir C. Wilson, and satisfaction at gallant rescue of his party."

POSTSCRIPT.

WITH the exception of the brief message of the 29th December 1884, "Kartoum all right, and can hold out for years," the last authentic news of the siege of Khartum is contained in General Gordon's Journal, which closes on the 14th December 1884.[1] His last words are: "Now MARK THIS,—if

---

[1] An interesting paper, by Lieutenant-Colonel Kitchener, R.E., which gives a full account of the last days of the siege, from native sources, has been published in the daily press under the title, "Notes on the Fall of Khartoum." The only point upon which I differ from Colonel Kitchener is the question of Faraj Pasha's treachery. I believe that he did facilitate the entry of the Mahdi's troops on the morning of the 26th January; but I believe also, that after the 25th December, or at any rate after the 31st December, Khartum could not have resisted a determined assault.

the expeditionary force, and I ask for no more than two hundred men, does not come in ten days, *the town may fall;* and I have done my best for the honour of our country. Good-bye." In his private letters, dated the same day, General Gordon stated that a crisis might occur at any time after Christmas-day. The crisis would naturally arrive when the provisions were finished; and we know, from his letter of the 4th November, that he did not expect them to last much longer than the 14th December.

From Christmas-day 1884 to the 26th January 1885, the garrison lived on coarse bread made from the pith of the palm-tree, on gum, and on a little tobacco. The fact that General Gordon was able to induce, not only the garrison, but the civilians in the city, to hold out for a month under such conditions, is one of the most remarkable features of his defence of Khartum, and affords the strongest proof of his wonderful influence over natives of all classes. During this period we have, through natives, occasional glimpses of General Gordon's unceasing vigilance, of his constant visits to the ramparts, of his firmness in resisting all overtures to surrender to the Mahdi, and of the way in which he kept up the spirits of his starving soldiers by proclamations announcing the speedy arrival of the relief expedition.

The Mahdi was fully aware of the straits to which the garrison was reduced, and waited quietly for the time when it would have to surrender without fighting, from want of food. When he heard of Sir Herbert Stewart's occupation of Jakdul he closed upon Omdurman, which had been cut off from all communication with Khartum, except by telegraph, on the 3d November. The precise date of the fall of Omdurman is not known; but, comparing the statements that have been received from different sources, it must have been some day between the 6th and 13th January. The commandant, Faraj Bey Allah, surrendered when his food came to an end. According to one account, he tried to march in square to the steamers which had been sent to withdraw him, but had to retire and lay down his arms. Faraj Bey and his garrison were well treated by the Mahdi; and this policy was not without its effect on the fate of Khartum, for a promise of similar treatment was held out to General Gordon's soldiers as an inducement to surrender without fighting.

The loss of Omdurman must have been a severe blow to the beleaguered garrison, as it appears to have been soon followed by a closer investment of the city. On Saturday, the 17th January, the day of Abu Klea, General Gordon made his last sortie; his troops were at first successful, but, reinforcements coming up on the Mahdi's side, they were driven back with a loss of 200 men. On the 20th January the Mahdi heard of the defeat of his troops at Abu Klea; and on the 22d, of the result of the fight at Gubat. On receipt of this news he appears to have written to General Gordon, and also to have sent letters to Faraj Pasha and his other partisans in the city, announcing the defeat of the English, and offering the garrison the same terms as those granted to the defenders of Omdurman. On the 23d, General Gordon had occasion to find serious fault with Faraj Pasha, and during the altercation that followed he is said to have struck him. This possibly had some influence in deciding Faraj Pasha to accept the Mahdi's terms, and he appears never to have been reconciled to General Gordon afterwards. On the 24th a council was held at the Palace to discuss the terms offered by the Mahdi.

Some of the members were in favour of accepting them, but General Gordon declared that he would hold out to the last and never surrender.[1] During the evening of the same day it was known at Omdurman that the steamers had left Gubat, and this news probably determined the Mahdi to attack next night. It is evident, from the various accounts received, that the Mahdi had made up his mind to try and take Khartum before the arrival of the English; and there is little doubt that if the steamers had left Gubat at an earlier date he would have attacked as soon as he heard they were on their way up, and the result would have been the same. The soldiers, weakened by famine, were in no condition to resist an assault; and it seems

---

[1] Rumours of the British successes appear to have been current in Khartum on the 23d and 24th; and General Gordon is said to have been aware of the arrival of troops on the Nile near Matammeh.

clear, from what we now know, that the Mahdi might have taken Khartum any time after Christmas - day; he hoped to starve the place out, and put off the assault to the last moment.[1]

On the 25th, General Gordon does not appear to have left the Palace, but he transacted business with several people, and one man, a Copt, states that he saw him there six hours after sunset. Before daylight on the 26th the Arabs attacked the lines of Khartum at the Messalamia Gate, and met with little or no resistance. Part of the attacking force seems to have passed between Fort Mogrim and the White Nile, over ground left dry by the fall of the river; whilst part crossed the ditch, according to one account, by filling it up with

[1] Hussein Pasha Khalifa, who was in the Mahdi's camp at Omdurman, states that the Mahdi was alarmed when he heard of Abu Klea, and consequently expedited the attack on Khartum.

straw, native beds, &c., which the men
carried with them as they advanced to the
assault ; or according to another account,
by filling it up during the night, with the
connivance of Faraj Pasha and Behnasawi
Bey, commanding the troops in that quarter.
The city was soon in the hands of the
Arabs, who for about three hours killed
every one they met ; a crier then went
round proclaiming the *Aman* or general
amnesty, but many Shagiyeh were killed
two days afterwards. Some black soldiers
held out at the Buri Gate until they saw
Khartum was in the hands of the Arabs,
and the garrison on Tuti Island did not surrender until mid-day. Lieutenant-Colonel
Kitchener, in his "Notes on the Fall of
Khartoum," does not credit the accusation
of treachery brought against Faraj Pasha ;
but, amongst Arabs, the first account of
an event is frequently correct, and I think
the story I heard on the evening of the

28th January is probably true.   The names
of Faraj Pasha and Behnasawi Bey have
been consistently connected with the act
of treachery ; and I believe that these men,
who commanded the troops at the Messalamia Gate, knew that an assault was going
to be made during the night of the 25th-
26th, and that they purposely neglected to
take any precautions to resist it ; they probably encouraged the soldiers to leave the
lines, and go into the city to search for
food.[1] Faraj Pasha was killed after the capture of Khartum, but Behnasawi Bey was
afterwards in high favour with the Mahdi.

---

[1] Before General Gordon's arrival at Khartum, a dep-
utation, headed by Muhammed Bey el Jazuli, had visited
the Mahdi at Rahad, and presented to him letters and
petitions, signed by persons of all classes at Khartum,
begging an assurance of safety, and expressing readiness
to submit. Throughout the siege there appears, from
General Gordon's Journal, to have been an influential
section of the people in favour of the Mahdi, and an act
of treachery such as that attributed to Faraj Pasha is not
surprising under the circumstances.

Of General Gordon's death we have two
independent accounts, which in all essen-
tial particulars agree with each other, and
appear to be trustworthy.   One of these, a
Cavass, who was in the service of Ibrahim
Bey Rushdi, came across the desert from
Omdurman ; the other was one of our own
messengers, who was in Khartum when it
fell, and came *viâ* Matammeh.   The Cavass,
who states that he was an eyewitness, says :
" On hearing the noise, I got my master's
donkey, and went with him to the Palace.
We met Gordon Pasha at the outer door of
the Palace.   Muhammed Bey Mustafa, with
my master, Ibrahim Bey Rushdi, and about
twenty Cavasses, then went with Gordon
towards the house of the Austrian Consul,
Hansal, near the church, when we met some
rebels in an open space near the outer gate of
the Palace.   Gordon Pasha was walking in
front, leading the party.   The rebels fired
a volley, and Gordon was killed at once ;

nine of the Cavasses, Ibrahim Bey Rushdi,
and Muhammed Bey Mustafa, were killed,
the rest ran away." The messenger was
not present, but went to the Palace soon
after sunrise; his statement is : " Faraj
Pasha withdrew the soldiers from the gate
near the White Nile, and allowed the rebels
to enter. Wad en Nejumi and Khalifa Ali
led the way; every one was asleep, and
before the sun rose the town was full of
Arabs. Some went to the Palace and met
Gordon, attended by some of his guard, at
the gate. Gordon fired his revolver, and
the rebels firing a volley killed Gordon
immediately. I saw Gordon lying dead
near the Palace gate." It is not unlikely
that General Gordon, when he heard that
the Arabs had entered the city, tried to
reach the church where the ammunition
was stored, and that he intended either to
try and hold out there until the relief

expedition arrived, or to blow up the magazine and prevent its falling into the Mahdi's hands. General Gordon was killed a few moments after he had quitted the Palace gate, and, according to the barbarous custom of the Sudan, his head appears to have been cut off and exposed at Omdurman. One man declares that he saw General Gordon's body, with the head on, some days after the fall of Khartum; but it is to be feared that the general evidence of the men who have escaped since the capture is correct.

The siege of Khartum lasted for 317 days—only nine days less than the great siege of Sevastopol, in which General Gordon first saw active service. For more than ten long weary months the wild tribes of the Sudan were kept in check by the genius, the indomitable resolution, and fertile resources of one man; and, long

after the controversies of the present day
have been forgotten, the defence of Khartum by General Gordon will be looked
upon as one of the most memorable military achievements of modern times.

APPENDIX.

APPENDIX I.

Letter from GENERAL GORDON to LORD WOLSELEY.

"KARTOUM, 4/11/84.

"Post came in yesterday from Debbah, Kitchener, dated 14th October, cipher letter from Lord Wolseley, 20th September last, which I cannot decipher, for Colonel Stewart took the cipher with him.

"No other communications have been received here since 31st, letter which arrived 17th September, a week after Colonel Stewart's steamer left this. On other side are names of Europeans who went with Colonel Stewart in steamer. At Metammah, waiting your orders, are five steamers with nine guns.

T

"We can hold out forty days with ease; after that it will be difficult.

"Terrible about loss of steamer.

"I sent Colonel Stewart, Power, and Herbin down, telling them to give you all information.

"With Colonel Stewart was the journal of all events from 1st March to the 10th September. The steamer carried a gun, and had a good force on board.

"The Mahdi is here, about eight miles away. All north side along the White Nile is free of Arabs; they are on south and south-west and east of town some way off; they are quiet.

"Senaar is all right, and knows of your coming.

"With steamers are my journals from 10th September to date, with all details, and map of Berber.

"We have occasional fights with Arabs.

"Mahdi says he will not fight during this month, Moharram.

"With him are all the Europeans, nuns, &c.; rumoured all are become Mussulman. Slatin is there; Lupton, Mahdi says, has surrendered.

"Since 10th March we have had up to date, exclusive of Kitchener's, 14th October, only two despatches: one, Dongola, with no date; one from Suakin, 5th May; one of some [? same] import, 27th April.

"I have sent out a crowd of messengers in all directions during eight months.

"Get the newspapers to say I received letters through Kitchener from Sir S. Baker, my sister, Stanley, from Congo. Do not send any more letters private—it is too great a risk. Do not write in cipher, for I have none, and it is of no import, for Mahdi knows everything, and you need not fear him.

"I should take the road from Ambukol to Metammah, where my steamers wait for you. Leontides, Greek Consul-General; Hauswell, Austrian Consul, all right.

"Stewart, Power, and Herbin went down in the 'Abbas.'

. "A letter came from Mitzakis, the 31st July, from Adowa.

"The messenger had a letter from King for me, but Mahdi captured it. Please explain that to his Majesty.

"If journal is lost with Stewart we have no record of events from the 1st March to the 10th September, except a journal kept by doctor.

"Your expedition is for relief of garrison, which I failed to accomplish. I decline to agree that it is for me personally.

" Stewart's journal was a gem, illustrated with all the Arabic letters of Mahdi to me, &c.

" You may not know what has passed here.

" The Arabs camped outside Khartoum on the 12th March. We attacked them on the 16th March ; got defeated, and lost heavily, also a gun. We then from that date had continual skirmishes with Arabs. Stewart was wounded slightly in arm.

" On one occasion when river rose we drove off Arabs in three or four engagements, and fired their towns. Sent up to Senaar two expeditions ; had another fight, and again was defeated with heavy loss ; the square was always broken. This last defeat was on the 4th September ; since then we have had comparative quiet.

" We fired 3,000,000 rounds.

" The Palace was the great place for the firing. Arabs have the Krupps here, and often have hulled our steamers. Arabs captured two small steamers at Berber, and one on Blue Nile. We have built two new ones, steamers. The steamers had bulwarks, and were struck with bullets 1090 times each on an average, and three times with shot each. We defended the lines with wire entanglements, and live shells as mines, which did great execution. We put lucifer-matches to ignite them.

"The soldiers are only half a month in arrears. We issue paper money, and also all the cloth in magazines. All the captives with Mahdi are well; the nuns, to avoid an Arab marriage, are ostensibly married to Greeks. Slatin is with Mahdi, and has all his property, and is well treated; but I hear to-day he is in chains. A mysterious Frenchman is with Mahdi, who came from Dongola.

"We have got a decoration made and distributed, with a grenade in centre; three classes— gold, silver, pewter.

"Kitchener says he has sent letters, and got none in reply. I have sent out during last month at least ten. Steamer with this leaves to-morrow for Metammah.

"Do not let any Egyptian soldiers come up here; take command of steamers direct, and turn out Egyptian fellaheen.

"If capture of steamer with Stewart is corroborated, tell French Consul-General that Mahdi has the cipher he gave Herbin.

"Hassan Effendi, telegraph clerk, was with Stewart. You should send a party to the place to investigate affairs, and take the steamer."

N.B.—On the back of the letter there was a

plan showing the distribution, round Khartum,
of the Mahdi's force of 20,000 men, and the
number and position of his guns.   There was
also a list of the Greeks who left Khartum in
the 'Abbas' with Colonel Stewart.

APPENDIX II.

Extracts from SIR HERBERT STEWART'S Instructions.

" On the 8th (January) you will arrange to start
yourself with the following force. . . .

" After such rest (at Jakdul) as your animals
require, you will proceed to Matammeh with the
following force. . . .

" On reaching Abu Klea you will establish a
post there, garrisoned by from 50 to 100 men
Sussex Regiment, as the nature of the ground
may require. . . .

" You will then advance on Matammeh, which
you will attack and occupy.   For this it may be
advisable to laager your convoy at the wells of
Shebacat.

"Having occupied Matammeh, you will leave there the Guards Camel Regiment, the detachment Sussex Regiment, the Naval Brigade, detachment Royal Engineers, and three guns Royal Artillery, . . . and return with the convoy to Jakdul. . . .

"On your return to Jakdul you will continue to forward stores by convoy to Matammeh. . . .

"Sir C. Wilson has been directed to show you his instructions. He will be in command of Matammeh when you leave."

APPENDIX III.

Organisation of the SUDAN CAMEL CORPS.

Guards Camel Regiment.

In Command—Lieutenant-Colonel Hon. E. E. T. Boscawen, Coldstream Guards.

Adjutant — Lieutenant O. Crutchley, Scots Guards.

Two officers and 43 non-commissioned officers and privates from the 1st, 2d, and 3d battalions Grenadier Guards; the 1st and 2d battalions Coldstream Guards; the 1st and 2d battalions Scots Guards; and 4 officers and 86 men the Royal Marines; 1 surgeon.

Total—21 officers, 387 non-commissioned officers and men.

Heavy Camel Regiment.

In Command—Lieutenant-Colonel Hon. R. A. J. Talbot, 1st Life Guards.

Adjutant—Captain Lord St Vincent, 16th Lancers.

Two officers and 43 non-commissioned officers and men from the 1st and 2d Life Guards; the Royal Horse Guards; the 2d, 4th, and 5th Dragoon Guards; the 1st and 2d Dragoons; and the 5th and 16th Lancers; 1 surgeon.

Total—23 officers, 430 non-commissioned officers and men.

Light Camel Regiment.

In Command—Colonel Stanley Clarke, half-pay.

Adjutant—Captain Paget, 7th Hussars.

Two officers and 43 non-commissioned officers and men from the 3d, 4th, 7th, 10th, 11th, 15th, 18th, 20th, and 21st Hussars; 1 surgeon.

Total—21 officers, 387 non-commissioned officers and men.

Mounted Infantry Camel Regiment.

In Command—Major Hon. G. H. Gough, 14th Hussars.

Twenty-three officers and 430 non-commissioned officers and men from various regiments ; 1 surgeon.

Grand total—88 officers, 1634 non-commissioned officers and men.

APPENDIX IV.

Letter from MUHAMMED EL KHEIR, Emir of Berber, to MUHAMMED ZEIN.   Picked up on the field of Abu Klea, January 17, 1885.

" In the name of God, the Merciful, the Compassionate.   Praise be to God, the Bountiful Ruler, and blessings be upon our Lord Muhammed and on his people.   From the servant of God, Muhammed el Kheir Abdullah Khojali, the Emir of the Imam, the Mahdi, on whom be peace, over all Berber and its territories, to his beloved, the Emir

Muhammed Zein Walad esh Sheikh, God prosper him. Amen.

"My beloved,—After peace, we inform you that your letter, and the letter of the Emir Sad Salim, have been received, and that their contents are known to us. God requite you with good, O my friends. It behoves you to get ready with energy and activity, and to carry on the holy war against the enemies of the faith, and to fight against the heathen, and the believers in more than one God. You must be patient and steadfast, and make raids. As our beloved, the Emir Sad Salim, has asked you for reinforcements, and sought your aid for victory, therefore give him reinforcements and help him to victory. Go to him with all the men of your Emirate. God Almighty has said, 'If they (the believers) seek your aid to ensure the victory of the faith, it is your duty to aid them;' and the Prophet, on whom be peace and blessings, has said, 'The believers are like a building—one part strengthens the other.' Therefore, on receipt of this letter, proceed with all your followers to the Emir Sad Salim, and do not wait for your ammunition, for you are not to fight the enemies of God with ammunition, but with spears and swords. Take therefore the equipment you have with you, and proceed to your brother, the Emir Sad Salim,

at once and without delay. This day all the
Emirs, the allies, and agents have been instructed
by letter to move over to the western side (of the
Nile). Peace.

(Sealed)   "MUHAMMED EL KHEIR
WALAD ABDULLAH.

"18th *Rabia el Awwal,*
4th *January* 1885.

"*P.S.*—Warn all your followers to take their
water-skins, their leathern sacks, and food for the
road; for if you meet the enemies of God, it will
be in the desert, and not in houses. Every one
must take his travelling equipment. This is the
time to sacrifice wealth and life in the cause
of God. You must obey the command of the
Almighty, and fight the good fight at the sacrifice
of your wealth and your lives. Be of good cheer;
great victory and much plenty await you, for God
has promised it to you, O ye congregations of
believing Moslems.

(Sealed)   "MUHAMMED EL KHEIR
WALAD ABDULLAH.

" 18th *Rabia el Awwal,*
4th *January* 1885."

APPENDIX V.

Instructions to COLONEL SIR C. WILSON, K.C.M.G., C.B., Royal Engineers.

"CAMP, KORTI, 7th *January* 1885.

"1. You will accompany the column under the command of Brigadier - General Sir Herbert Stewart, K.C.B., which will leave Korti to-morrow for Matammeh.

"Your intimate knowledge of Soudan affairs will enable you to be of great use to him during his operations away from these headquarters.

"2. You will endeavour to enter into friendly relations with the Hassaniyeh tribe, and to induce them, if possible, to carry supplies for us across the desert, and to sell us sheep, cattle, &c.

"3. As soon as Matammeh is in our occupation, Sir H. Stewart will despatch a messenger to Korti with an account of his march, &c.; and you will be good enough to send me by same opportunity all political information you may have obtained, all news of General Gordon, the so-called Mahdi, &c.

"4. I am sending Captain Lord Charles Beresford, R.N., with a small party of seamen, to ac-

company Sir H. Stewart to Matammeh, where,
if there are any steamers, Lord Charles Beresford
will take possession of one or two of them, as he
may think best. Any Egyptian (fellaheen) soldiers on them can be converted into camel-drivers,
and come back here with unloaded camels.

" 5. As soon as Lord Charles Beresford reports
that he is ready to proceed with one or more
steamers to Khartoum, you will go to that place
with him, and deliver the enclosed letter to
General Gordon. I leave it open so that you
may read it.

" 6. Orders have been given to Sir H. Stewart
to send a small detachment of infantry with you
to Khartoum. If you like, you can, upon arriving
there, march these men through the city to show
the people that British troops are near at hand.
If there is any epidemic in town you will not
do this. I do not wish them to sleep in the
city. They must return with you to Matammeh.
You will only stay in Khartoum long enough to
confer fully with General Gordon. Having done
so, you will return with Lord Charles Beresford
in steamers to Matammeh.

" 7. My letter to General Gordon will explain
to you the object of your mission. You will
confer with him both upon the military and upon

the political position. You are aware of the great difficulty of feeding this army at such a great distance from the sea. You know how we are off in the matter of supplies, the condition and distribution of the troops under my command, the dates when Major-General Earle will be able to move on Abu-Ahmed, &c.

"8. I am sending with you the three officers named in the margin,[1] who will accompany you to Khartoum, and will remain there to assist General Gordon until I am able to relieve that place.

"9. It is always possible that when Mohamed Achmet fully realises that an English army is approaching Khartoum he will retreat, and thus raise the siege. Khartoum would under such circumstances continue to be the political centre of our operations, but Berber would become our military objective. No British troops would be sent to Khartoum beyond a few red-coats in steamers for the purpose of impressing on the inhabitants the fact that it was to the presence of our army they owed their safety.

"The siege of Khartoum being thus raised, all

---

[1] Major Dickson, Royal Dragoons ; Lieutenant Stuart-Wortley, Royal Rifles ; the third to be named on arrival at Matammeh.

our military arrangements would be made with a view to the immediate occupation of Berber, and to a march across the desert to Ariab, on the Suakin road.

"10. Upon arrival at Matammeh, it is very possible you may find papers or letters from General Gordon awaiting us. You will be good enough to send them to me by the first messenger coming here.

"Upon your return to Matammeh from Khartoum you will rejoin my headquarters at your earliest possible convenience.

(Signed) "WOLSELEY, *General.*"

The above instructions were accompanied by the following paper, giving the dates referred to in paragraph 7 :—

"DEPUTY ADJUTANT-GENERAL.

"The following is my estimate of approximate times :—

"General Earle's force should, with luck, be in a position to commence its forward movement on the 20th January.

"The whole of that force should have moved by the 25th January.

" It will, I hope, reach Abu-Ahmed about the 10th February, Berber about the 22d February, and Shendy about the 5th March.

" I have not calculated on its meeting with any serious opposition before Berber.

" Lord Wolseley's force will commence to reach Matammeh the 16th January, and should be concentrated there with sixty days' supplies by the 2d March.   If we hire many camels this date may be anticipated.

" REDVERS BULLER,
Major-General.

" *8th January* 1885."

APPENDIX VI.

Approximate Distribution of Troops in the Desert
on the 8th January 1885.

Sir H. Stewart's column :—

	Officers.	N.-C. Officers and Men.
Staff, ...	8	6
Naval Brigade, ...	5	53
19th Hussars, ...	9	121
Heavy Camel Regiment, . .	24	376

	Officers.	N.-C. Officers and Men.
Mounted Infantry Camel Regiment, ...	21	336
Royal Artillery, ...	4	39
Royal Sussex Regiment, . .	16	401
Essex Regiment, . . .	3	55
Commissariat and Transport, .	5	72
Medical Staff, ...	3	50
Total, . .	98	1509

In addition to the above there were 304 natives, 2228 camels, and 155 horses.

Colonel Stanley Clarke's convoy *en route* for Jakdul :—

10 officers and 106 men of the Light Camel Regiment, and 1120 camels.

At the Wells of Howeiyat :—

Mounted Infantry Camel Regiment—3 officers, 30 men, and 33 camels.

At Jakdul :—

	Officers.	Men.
Guards Camel Regiment, . . .	19	365
Royal Engineers, ...	2	25
Medical Staff, ...	1	10
	22	400

And 20 camels.

The detachment of the Essex Regiment was left at Howeiyat, and the Mounted Infantry went on with Sir H. Stewart's column. The Guards

Camel Regiment at Jakdul was relieved by a strong detachment of the Royal Sussex, and went on with the column to Abu Klea.

APPENDIX VII.

GENERAL GORDON to the Officer Commanding H.M. Troops.

"KARTOUM, 20 *Oct.* '84.

"Sir,—I have sent the steamers 'Saphia,' 'Mansourah,' 'Bordeen,' 'Talataween,' 'Tewfikia,' down towards Berber, to aid you. On board these steamers are officers and men of Egyptian army. I request :—

"1. You will take charge of the steamers (though I would not recommend you to change the captains, the *reis* or steersmen, or the crews).

"2. That you will take out of those steamers all Egyptian officers and soldiers. I make you a present of these *hens*, and request you will not let one come back here to me. I include in this list of prescribed all ranks, Pachas, Beys, &c., &c.

"3. I request YOU will take charge of these

steamers, and not allow any nominee of Tewfik Pacha to interfere with you in this matter.

"The officers and soldiers of Egypt have been paid, or their pay has been regulated, so you will have no difficulty on that score.

"If you do not use the steamers, at least take out the *hens* and send them back empty.

"You will find that the steamers are well supplied with ammunition, &c.

"If you choose to put black troops on board, they will be welcome, but not these heroes of Tel-el-Kebir.—I have the honour to be, Sir, your obedient servant,   C. G. GORDON.

"Officer Commanding
    H. M. Troops."

APPENDIX VIII.

Letter addressed by MUHAMMED AHMED to the British and Shagiyeh officers on board the steamers returning from Khartum. Dated 11 Rabia the second, 1302 (January 28th 1885).

"In the name of God the Merciful, the Compassionate. Praise be to the Bountiful Sovereign, and blessings be upon our Lord Muhammed and on his family. From the servant who stands in need of God, and on whom he places dependence, Muhammed the Mahdi, son of Abdullah, to the British and Shagiyeh officers, and their followers: —God direct them to the truth. Surrender and you will be spared. Do not disobey, else you will rue it. And I will briefly inform you, perchance God Almighty may put you upon the path of the righteous. Know then that the city of Khartum and its surroundings are like the garrison of a stronghold; God has destroyed it and other places by our hands; nothing can withstand His power and might; and by the bounty of God all has come into our hands. As you have become a small remnant, like a leaflet, within our grasp, two alternatives are offered to you. If you surrender and prevent the shedding of your blood and the blood of God's creatures who are under your leadership, well and good: grace and security from God and His Prophet, and security from us will be upon you. But if you do not believe what we have said, and desire to ascertain the truth of the killing of Khartum,[1] send a special envoy on

---

[1] The Mahdi's letter bears traces of having been hurriedly written, and "Khartum" has been erroneously written for "Gordon," as the word translated "killing" is only used for killing a man or animal.

your part to see the truth of what we say: and
to your envoy is given the security of God and
His Prophet, till he comes to us and sees and
returns under a guard from us, to see and be
warned of God, even as God says: ' If any one
of the polytheists seek help of thee, help him that
he may learn the word of God Almighty.'   You
are offered the alternative of fighting or surren-
dering to the command of God, and returning
unto Him.   Were it not for pity for you we
would not write. to you in this manner; and if
you pay heed, on receipt of this my letter to you,
fear nothing, for nothing will happen to you after
the (granting) of the security of God and His
Prophet to you; but if you refuse you shall taste
evil, in that you turn away from the pathway
of God to the torment of the other world.   For
it is known that victory is unto the believers,
even as God has promised them in His revealed
Book.   Do not be deceived and put confidence
in your steamers and other things, and delay
deciding until you rue it; but rather hasten to
your benefit and profit before your wings are cut.
Much reasoning will not convert; for it is God
who converts, and He who lets go astray, and
thou wilt find no ruler over Him.   What has been

said is enough for him who has been reached by Providence.

	There is no God but God ; Muhammed is the Prophet of God. MUHAMMED, the Mahdi, son of Abdullah, 1293.[1]
(Sealed)	

APPENDIX IX.

1. MUHAMMED AHMED, the Mahdi, son of Abdullah, to KHASHM EL MUS, and the Soldiers on the steamers, dated 18th Moharrem 1302 (6th November 1884).

Extract.

"Do not think I seek your property. If you surrender you will be forgiven. I am the expected Mahdi, the successor of your Prophet. He who does not believe in me and follow me shall suffer in this world and the next. I am promised the kingdom of all the earth. You have seen my victories whilst weak and poor. Now I have the arms taken from Rashid Bey, Wad Shalalu, and

[1] This is the date of the cutting of the seal; it is probably antedated, as Muhammed Ahmed had not declared his mission in 1293.

Hicks. I desire that my friends should obtain grace. I write this because I think well of you."

2. AHMED MUSTAFA, son of El Feki el Amin, and
   others, to the MELIK KHASHM EL MUS, dated
   6th Safar 1302 (24th November 1884).

Extract.

" I take pity on you, and wish you to remain with people of your own race, and to be counted amongst those who are worthy of happiness and of the followers of God, His Prophet, and His Mahdi. Although you have fought against the allies of God, yet the Mahdi will forgive you. Beware of disregarding the advice of the Mahdi, on whom be peace ; and beware of fighting against God, His Prophet, and His Mahdi. If you do not return from your evil ways, God will destroy you by the hand of the Mahdi," &c.

3. AHMED MUSTAFA, and others, to their beloved
   friends KHASHM EL MUS and the Soldiers on
   the steamers, dated 1st Rabia, II. 1302 (18th
   January 1885).

Extract.

" May God repay you for what you have done.

Choose a place of meeting, either opposite this place or at Kubbet Wad Barrah, and fix an hour for the interview. Trust in God, be firm in your resolution, and fear nothing. The English were destroyed yesterday; so come quickly and save your lives, your property, and your children. Send Abd ul Faraj to inform us of the place and hour of the meeting."

APPENDIX X.

1. MUHAMMED EL MABAESI and MUHAMMED MANSUR to KHASHM EL MUS, ABD UL HAMID, and MUHAMMED ABUD, dated 15th Rabia the second, 1302 (1st February 1885).

" You are aware that we have been trying to save you, and yet you are trying to destroy yourselves. After the wreck of the steamer yesterday you sent a boat to Matammeh to call the English to your assistance. Should the boat be destined to get there safely, and should the English come and take you with them to Europe, Rome, and Constantinople, remember that we shall conquer all the same, as it has been foretold by our Prophet; peace be unto him. If you live long enough you will see the troops of the Mahdi spreading over Europe, Rome, and Constantinople, after which there will be nothing left for you but hell and damnation."

2. HASSAN WAD KHALID and SAID WAD EL SAID to KHASHM EL MUS and ABD UL HAMID, dated 15th Rabia 1302 (1st February 1885).

Précis.

Counsels and advises them to surrender, and promises that no harm will be done to them for having fought against the Mahdi. States that the Mahdi is merciful, and will grant them a general pardon.

THE END.

www.ingramcontent.com/pod-product-compliance
Lightning Source LLC
Chambersburg PA
CBHW020807100426
42814CB00014B/363/J